Why A Good God Allows Bad Things to Happen

by Dr. Dave Arnold

Why A Good God Allows Bad Things to Happen
by Dr. Dave Arnold

Printed in the United States of America

ISBN 9781622306732

www.xulonpress.com

Bob:

May this book be a
blessing to you!

"It has often been pointed out that a fundamental requirement in expounding the word of God is a need of preserving the balance of truth. With this we are in hearty accord. Two things are beyond dispute: God is sovereign, man is responsible. ... There is real danger of overemphasizing the one and ignoring the other, we readily admit; and history furnishes numerous examples of both. To emphasize the sovereignty of God, without also maintaining the accountability of the creature, tends to fatalism; to be so concerned in maintaining the responsibility of man, as to lose sight of the sovereignty of God, is to exalt the creature and dishonor the creator."[1]

A.W. Pink

---

[1] Pink, A.W.; The Sovereignty of God. The Banner of Truth Trust. London, Great Britian, 1928. p 9.

❦

"I just finished reading the book this morning; and I hasten to tell you that it warmed my heart. You approach God's sovereign will over a life in a warm and personal way by using your own testimony to illustrate the truths you expound.

The book is very practical and straightforward and to me, its big appeal is that it deals with a deep theological reality in a manner in which the layman can be thoroughly engaged. You don't talk over a reader's head, but you involve him/her in a heart-to-heart discourse about God's sovereignty as it plays out in his daily life. Thank you Dave!"

Dr. Bob Jones III
President Emeritus
Bob Jones University

"The sovereignty of God speaks to His ultimate power. It declares absolute ascendancy. The one with sovereign powers has all authority. This is the God that Evangelist/ Missionary David Arnold describes. This volume comes from the heart of a man who has experienced that which he writes about. He shares about the work and direction of God in his ministry and personal life. As you read this book you will be refreshed at the way God works. Thank you, Dave, for reminding me and refreshing all of us about a foundational truth of our God. He is sovereign. Glory be to Him."

Dr. Dino J. Pedrone

President

Davis College

Dedication

It is with much love and appreciation to two special ladies in my life. First, to my wife Gloria of 51 years. Gloria has been a very special influence in my life in many ways. She led me to the Lord and helped to refresh my spirit from time to time. With the right words to help me keep on keeping on. She has been a wonderful teacher in a Christian school for almost 40 years and to this day we have many coming to thank her for her influence in their lives. She has been a great mother to my three children, David, Rebecca, and Peter. A faithful pastors wife for 15 years and now for the last 30 years an encouragement in my work of evangelism and missions. Much of my ministry would not have had the blessing of God on it had it not been for her dedication to the Lord and to me. Thanks you Gloria.

To my daughter, Rebecca, who through her special skills and love for her father kept me on track of reaching my goals when at times I felt like the tasks were much greater than my ability. Rebecca was twice given to me by God. Due to the fact that at birth she weighed 1 lb. 6 oz. and the attending physicians said she would not live and if she did would be severely handicapped. God intervened and gave us back our daughter and she too has been an influence to help me keep on keeping on. Thank you Becky.

Summary from the Author

My friends this book was born in the heart of a pastor who was forced at times to watch some of his best, most faithful church members enter into the University of suffering. To me, in most cases, people who deserved the better portions of life. However, I would conclude, in an effort to comfort my own thoughts, this must be the will of God for them. But God Why? How was I to answer these people when I knew they would soon be coming asking questions, trying to make sense out of what seemed to be nonsense. Now I had the awesome responsibility of even defending God.

This book was also born in the heart of a pastor who had to struggle with his own heartaches, personal loses, and rejection of friends. I had to wrestle with the feelings that God did not really care about me just like many of my church members. I had to learn to deal with fears, doubts, and bitterness towards church members and even towards God.

I am now an old man and I can tell you I have found the peace of God in these arenas and pray that you will too and that you will find the peace of God and learn to rest, "rest in the arms of Jesus".

Yours for Jesus' sake,

Dave Arnold

Table of Contents:

Preface. . . . . .page xv

Chapter 1 Kingdom Builders . . . . .page 19

Chapter 2 His Wonders to Perform. . . . . .page 25

Chapter 3 Sovereignty. . . . . .page 37

Chapter 4 Suffering. . . . . .page 57

Chapter 5 Service . . . . .page 77

Chapter 6 The War Zone. . . . . .page 80

Chapter 7 The Weary Christian Syndrome . . . . .page 106

God Moves In Mysterious Ways

God moves in a mysterious way
His wonders to perform;
He plants His footsteps in the sea,
And rides upon the storm.
Deep in unfathomable mines
Of never-failing skill
He treasures up His bright designs,
And works His sovereign will.
Ye fearful saints, fresh courage take,
The clouds ye so much dread
Are big with mercy, and shall break
In blessings on your head.
Judge not the Lord by feeble sense,
But trust Him for His grace;
Behind a frowning providence
He hides a smiling face.
His purposes will ripen fast,
Unfolding every hour;
The bud may have a bitter taste,
But sweet will be the flower.
Blind unbelief is sure to err,
And scan his work in vain;
God is His own interpreter,
And He will make it plain.
William Cowper

In 1 Corinthians 4:1-5, the Apostle Paul deals with a very critical and sensitive area in our walk with God. This arena is the mysterious ways in which God sometimes chooses to work. This book deals with a collage of these very strange and even at times perplexing treatments of a God Who tells us that he loves us and desires the best for us, which seems to be incongruous with His nature. From time to time, we have all heard people or even perhaps we have even uttered words such as this: "If God is truly in control of all things, why would he allow bad things, or even do bad things to humans? If this is how God works, then perhaps we don't like God at all."[2] In 1942 Albert Einstein, the most intellectual thinker of the 20th century, once invited four clergymen to come to his home for what he called "a spiritual tea party." He started the discussion by asking the clergy—which consisted of an Episcopalian Bishop, a Rabbi, a Church of England Bishop, and a Lutheran minister—"If God really is good, why is there so much evil in this world? If you tell me that the evil is outside of God's control and that God is not involved then, gentlemen, I would conclude that your God is not truly omniscient and that God is not God at all. If you say that He is involved but is willing to sit back and allow things that are bad to continue, then I see this God as not a loving God at all. If, in fact, you say He is involved and has created evil, then again I would not be interested in this kind of God because He is merely manipulating humankind and is indeed cruel."

The frustration and dilemma that disturbed Einstein was due to the news that had been leaking out of Germany concerning the slaughter of Jews. All Jews—men, women, and even children. Einstein was a Jew by birth. He had been told by his parents that the Jewish people were God's chosen people. If this were indeed true, he reasoned, that God must be

---

[2] Colson, Charles. How Now Shall We Live. Tyndale House Publisher. 1999. Page 206.

cold and heartless and totally unconcerned or even perhaps not omniscient enough to control the situation.

It is said that none of the clergy could give an answer to this scientist, who believed that every effect has an initial cause. If God is the cause, He is cruel. Or, if there is an effect beyond His omniscience, He is not God at all. Einstein dismissed the gathering by saying, "Perhaps gentlemen, I must look elsewhere for my answers. Religion is as confused as I am. There is a cause somewhere. I guess maybe it is in science after all."[3] It is in this perhaps unfathomable subject of the sovereignty of God that I launch my thoughts, hoping to bring some meaning and perhaps solid footing on this slippery slope of the human ability to explain God. May we together pull back the veil of finite understanding to peek into this university of suffering and see if we can identify Him in it all, not as a passive bystander, but as the omnipotent God that He truly is. I present to you *Why A Good God Allows Bad Things to Happen.*

[3] Ibid.

Chapter 1
Kingdom Builders

*These words spake Jesus, and lifted up His eyes to heaven,
and said, "Father, the hour is come; glorify thy Son, that
thy Son may also glorify thee."*

John 17:1

The Greek word for "glorify" is *doxa*, which means to give an expression of or an opinion of someone or something. It is in this high priestly prayer that Jesus is praying to the Father that those to whom the Father hath given to him would be willing, in this world, to give the proper expression of God in all things, even in suffering.

During my 45+ years of ministry, it has appeared to me that God has two major objectives in his overall design for mankind. In our Lord's great high priestly prayer found in John 17, we find that Jesus' major emphasis is building an eternal kingdom and is not as much concerned about an earthly one. In John 18:36 He said, *"My kingdom is not of this world."* My friend, we must ever keep that thought paramount in our minds or we will have a tendency to mistrust our sovereign God. You see, we get confused, which is only natural, because we see this world through the lens of this earthly journey. We must, by the grace of God, see this world through the lens of an eternal kingdom. Now, because God is focused on that eternal kingdom, in Jesus' prayer to the Father, he is praying that His people be willing to allow Him to use them to be kingdom builders. The rest of the prayer was concerning his kingdom builders. He prayed that God would sanctify His people(John 17:17). He prayed not that the Father would take His children out of the world, but that He would use them to influence the world. This sanctification will come about through suffering and difficult times. But all of these events are for the purpose of God, using many difficult and seemingly unfair methods to bring people to a saving knowledge of Jesus and to cause those whom He chooses to use to have a deeper, closer walk with God as he stated in closing. That just as the Father and Son are one, the Christian and his Lord may be one.

Perhaps the best way to convey the basis of this book would be to remind you of the poem that most of us have read as well as the picture called "Footprints in the Sand." It reveals to us, and reminds us, that we never walk alone; God walks before us and with us and sometimes is carrying us through troublesome times.

Footprints in the Sand

One night a man had a dream. He dreamed

he was walking along the beach with the LORD.

Across the sky flashed scenes from his life.

For each scene he noticed two sets of

footprints in the sand: one belonging

to him, and the other to the LORD.

When the last scene of his life flashed before him,

he looked back at the footprints in the sand.

He noticed that many times along the path of

his life there was only **one** set of footprints.

He also noticed that it happened at the very

lowest and saddest times in his life.

This really bothered him and he

questioned the LORD about it:

"LORD, you said that once I decided to follow

you, you'd walk with me all the way.

But I have noticed that during the most

troublesome times in my life,

there is only one set of footprints.

I don't understand why when

I needed you most you would leave me."

The LORD replied:

"My son, my precious child,

I love you and I would never leave you.

During your times of trial and suffering,

when you see only one set of footprints,

it was then that I carried you."

Mary Stevenson

It has been my purpose to show that no matter where we go or what we go through, "Our Jesus" has been there. In John 14:6 Jesus said, *"I am the way."*

He is a pattern for us and, if you will, our GPS (Global Positioning Satellite) to ultimately get us to where we should be. Thank God for a pattern, thank God for a map, and thank God for direction and guidance. He is assuring us that He is the one that is leading us and our responsibility is to keep our eyes on Him and follow Him.

As we take on this earthly pilgrimage, we will walk through some lonesome valleys and troublesome times. The one advantage we have as Christians is that we are never left without a pattern. We have had One who has gone before us. We will never find ourselves walking in an area where He has not been. Not only has He been there but He has been victorious there, even in the very Valley of Death.

We must also realize that not only do we have Jesus who has gone before us, but we have a great host of others who have laid down a pattern in which we may choose to walk as well. That is why the writer of the book of Hebrews says in chapter 12, verse 13, *"And make straight paths for your feet, lest that which is lame be turned out of the way; but let it rather be healed."* You see, we can only see Jesus through the eye of faith and through the Word.

Many of us conclude that we know *Jesus* can be victorious, but we doubt that *we* can. However, ever before us are those in the land of the living. It is because of them and their examples that I came to write this book. It is them that we can see, we can hear, and we can touch. In some

22

cases, it is easier to identify with them. It is because of them that we have a light on our pathway and a lamp before our feet.

The next and perhaps the most profound purpose for this book is to substantiate *why* it is that, "God works in mysterious ways His wonders to perform."[4] Perhaps the purpose is that our Sovereign God is creating a pattern that He intends to use to help those after us. The question we must be willing to settle before God once we are assured that this is God at work in our lives is, "Am I willing to let God use me as a pattern that I might help others?" So very often it is not about me, it is about others. You see, there is not only a great host *before* us, and a great company *with* us, but there is as well a multitude *which no man can number* coming *after* us. It is for their benefit as well as for our own that God leads us in strange and often in very difficult ways. We have been chosen by God to be counted worthy of being a pattern. You see, if I have never had a problem, how can I tell those behind me that God can help them? On their behalf, God is asking me to be careful of the pattern that I am laying down, to be careful of my footprints, and to be careful of my example, because I am being read and learned of by many men.

In this book I have chosen some illustrations, both of individuals and of nations that have profoundly captured my attention and have stirred my heart to do two things: First of all, to answer once and for all the age-old question we all ask: "Why, God?" Secondly, to show how, in all of these unanswerable questions of life, God was truly and infinitely working His wonders to perform.

---

[4] Cowper, William. God Moves In Mysterious Ways. Poem

Now, not for one moment am I suggesting that when you have finished this book, you will never have to ask "Why?" again, nor am I intimating that you will always see the pattern God is using *you* to lay down. My only intention in writing this book is to be once again reminded that God is always at work and always has an ultimate and perfect purpose.

I also desire that as you read these illustrations, they will challenge you to be the example, pattern and pathway that God wants you to be, so that you ultimately will lead those who are behind you to the glorious kingdom of God by making straight paths for your feet.

Chapter 2
His wonders to perform

Jesus said, "I am the way."

The Christian life is referred to by the writers of the Holy Scriptures, as well as by others, in various and interesting ways. For instance, some refer to it as a pilgrimage, others as a contest or a sporting event. Paul spoke of it as a great conflict, a warfare, a battle; in essence, a struggle between life and death.

Certainly all of these do indeed paint or portray in our minds' eye a fitting picture of our walk with God through this land of the living. Of all the descriptions, none seems to challenge or intrigue me more than the description that the people of Palestine gave to the followers of Jesus. They referred to the disciples of Jesus as "This Way People." "This Way" was first used by Saul of Tarsus as he tried to describe to the emperor the sect of people who were followers of Jesus. In Acts chapter 9, Saul desires to receive permission from the High Priest to go to Damascus and persecute and put into prison the heretics and deserters of the Jewish faith.

"This Way" was his way of describing them. Perhaps still indelible upon his mind was the martyrdom of the one called Stephen. Such a remarkable man he was. Why, even in the face of death, this disciple of Jesus never strayed from his convictions. Obviously Saul could never erase from his mind those dying words that were but a mere whisper on his fainting breath, "Father lay not this sin to their charge." How could one who was being martyred at the hands of men with no compassion be filled with such compassion? Truly this was a man with a set of values that not even the threat of death could cause him to abandon.

Perhaps, as Saul reflected on this scene from time to time and wished— oh how he wished—he could forget, he was convinced that these people had found a way in which to walk and would not change. So, when trying to describe them, he referred to them as people of "This Way." "This Way" of Stephen, "This Way" of conviction, "This Way" of compassion and forgiveness, "This Way" of great peace, even in the very face of adversity and ultimate death.

It was, as you remember, as Paul gave his testimony and presented his own defense before Governor Felix in Acts 24, that he once again reiterated him the consecration he had and the zeal he felt within his own heart to be faithful to his Lord Jesus. Then, as Felix sat and listened to this stirring testimony, he came under guilt of his own sin. The Scriptures say it was so intense that he began to tremble (verse 25). However, just like so many even to this day, he dismissed Paul and said, *"When I have a more convenient season or time, I will call you back and take up this matter again."* The great travesty of such a decision is that usually a convenient time never again arises… The devil will do all he can to see to it that this occasion of conviction never rises again. For Felix, it appears for all practical purposes that it never did return.

Then, as Paul was transferred to King Herod Agrippa II (the grandson of King Herod, the persecutor of Jesus), he once again reminded this king of the one who was the leader of this new sect of people. One called Jesus. As Agrippa sat and heard Paul recount the wonderful story of this one who came to seek and save that which was lost, the king said, *"Paul, almost thou persuadest me to be a Christian,"* (Acts 26:28).

You see, it was the way of the man Jesus that the disciples were copying. It was the way he walked among men, the way he had compassion for those for whom others had no compassion. It was "This Way" of Jesus that had literally captured the attention of all the known world of that day. Why, word had even reached over the sea to Rome. It was "This Way" of showing mercy that caused Jesus to stop one day at the side of a blind man ignored and made fun of by others and say to him, "Open your eyes and see."

But, most of all, it was "This Way" of patience and obedience that caused Jesus, when he was left alone in the garden, to pray to the Father that *If it were possible, let this cup pass from me*, but concluded by saying, *"Nevertheless, not my will, but thine be done,"* (Matthew 26:38). And then, just a few days later, Jesus showed his disciples as well as us how that even in death we are more than conquerors. *"For he hath made Him to be sin for us, who knew no sin; that we might be made the righteousness of God in Him"*(II Corinthians 5:21).

"This Way" was the pattern and example these early men were following. The blessed first-century Christians were not just in some random walk or, if you please, just doing their own thing. They were, in fact, walking in the footprints of Jesus. As we follow these footprints, we too

27

can turn aside from the path of temptation and sin. We can, in fact, walk victoriously through the path of rejection, the path of *pathos*, the path of suffering and, yes, even the awful path that leads to the very jaws of death. However, as we watch and study these dear pilgrims following Jesus, we see them walking with rejoicing and peace. We hear them say that they are so thankful that Jesus counted them worthy to walk where he walked. You also notice, as they walked in this path, that they had an incredible fellowship with their blessed Lord.

"This Way," beloved, is the same way that you and I have been called to follow. Remember, we are merely to follow the footprints set before us, the prints not only of Jesus but now of thousands and thousands of other pilgrims who have preceded us. That is why the writer of the book of Hebrews admonishes us to, *"Make straight paths for your feet, lest that which is lame be turned out of the way; but let it rather be healed. Follow peace with all men, and holiness, without which no man shall see the Lord,"* (Hebrews 12:13-14).

You see, as we follow "This Way," the very footprints of Jesus, and the footprints of many others, we have several major obligations and responsibilities:

(1) We must be born again. This born-again experience is the entrance into a new life of peace and power. Someone has said the world does not need more of anything but peace. Jesus is referred to as the Prince of Peace. Beloved, if men and women are deprived of everything but peace, they are still able to hold up and continue on. Peace can only come through an abiding fellowship with Christ. How often I have seen people of God go through

adversities and heartaches. I have wondered to myself how they will ever hold up. But, somehow, they do. When you see such an experience, it speaks volumes to your soul. You just know it is the working of God.

(2) We must keep our eyes on Jesus. I know this sounds a bit trite or simplistic, but it is the only solution to our pilgrimage. If we fail to do this, we will run the awful risk of side-stepping and getting off the path of His Way. This inevitably leads to a life of aimless wondering around in this wilderness of confusion, loneliness and sin; but, most importantly, we face the awful failure of not achieving God's ultimate plan and purpose for our lives. There are many Christians who are groping through this world without peace or direction and are of very little value to God or man. I want to plead with you who are reading these words, if you are away from the path, come back. Jesus longs for you to return. He loves you and died for you, and thank God, He never gives up on you. Listen to His cry for you: *"O Jerusalem* (Christian), *how often would I have gathered thy children* (YOU) *under my wings, but you would not,"* (Matthew 23:37). Oh, he does not delight in seeing you where you are. Yes, it was indeed the path of God that led you where you became discouraged. God does not just lead by still waters or deep green pastures, but be reminded His footprints do not stop at the waters' edge. His footprints go right on. All you have to do is follow. He has gone before you so that He can say, "I am the Way."

(3) We must be empowered. In this book I am not for one moment suggesting that what you must do is pull yourself up by your own boot straps and tough it out, or just persevere in keeping your nose to the grindstone. No, not at all.

29

What we are talking about in this book is the supernatural working of God that is absolutely necessary for peace and victory. None of us are sufficient in and of ourselves. We are all nothing more or less than dust. *"For he knoweth our frame; he remembereth that we are dust,"* (Psalms 103:14). Lurking within the depths of every human heart are the seeds for our own destruction. We will all, sooner or later, be very vulnerable to the testings and trials of life. Even that hard, arrogant, self-conceited, self-assertive one that feels he needs no one will one day come to the end of his own sufficiency.

Perhaps this is the place, the only place, where man is in a position to be converted or can hope to persevere. After all, as long as he is comfortable and in need of nothing, why should he come and follow anyone, let alone Jesus? But that hour will come. His testing is inevitable. I heard Woodrow Kroll of the "Back to the Bible" radio broadcast one day make this statement. "Men are either in a problem, coming out of a problem, or about to go into a problem." And then he said, "for this, we have Jesus." The tragedy is that men do not always turn to God. Many turn further away. Have you seen this? Have you experienced watching two people go through a similar experience; one seems to come closer to God and another one seems to be driven further from Him? The difference is that in that great hour of testing, the first one is able to find the peace of God and the strength of God to sustain him. For whatever reason, the other one is filled with resentment and self-pity and ultimately walks away from God. I have come to believe that in most of these unanswerable questions of life, it's really not so much about me as it is about others. The plan that God was developing in Stephen's case was really not so much about Stephen, but rather the man Saul, who had instigated the whole affair. Was Stephen merely used and abused while Saul would become the triumphant one? Not at all! God was elevating Stephen to an eternal reward called a Martyr's Crown, a congressional medal of honor, if you will. Romans 8:18 states, *"For I reckon that the sufferings of this present time are not worthy to be compared with the glory which shall be revealed in us."* I am thoroughly convinced that God does work in mysterious ways to bring us to the wonderful life in Christ. Perhaps as you read this book, that is the exact reason God has led you into the deep valley of life. He does not hate you. He does not delight in seeing you sad and confused. Why, even in your strength, you were no match for him. Perhaps this is His way of finally getting your attention. God is in the business of building an eternal kingdom, and He will do all He can to make you a part of the heavenly throng which will gather there. But, my friend, He will not superimpose his sovereignty over your free will. He wants you to love Him, and come to Him, and yield to Him.

This book is about people and nations who rose above their heartache, not because they were strong people, but because they had a strong hand on them that empowered them and gave them peace even in the midst of their storm.

To others of you who are saved, you have been led where you are. Certainly, you would probably never have chosen this lot in life. Why would anyone want or need such an awful hell as life sometimes is? I think of a pastor friend of mine. He has been faithful to God for many, many years. He and his dear wife, Winnie, labored together winning many people to Christ. Then, suddenly, it all came crashing down as Winnie was killed in a car accident on Valentine's Day. My friend, why, why, would a good God, a loving God, do or allow this? Was this God or are there things in life that happen, just accidents in which God is not involved? I pray that in this book I will be able to make some contribution that will be of help and cause us all to have hope in God.

I shall never forget the awful feeling, the sick feeling in the pit of my stomach, when I had to anticipate looking into this good man's eyes and say something I hoped and prayed would be right. Now, several years later, my friend, Rev. Ernie Moore, has had the heartache of having to bury his daughter who fought a courageous battle with cancer. He has to walk once again to that empty grave and lay to her eternal rest that which was so precious to his heart. I am convinced that Brother Moore must be a chosen vessel and one God could trust to walk this awful pathway. God is using him for the distinct reason that others, many others who would need his help and his example, would come to peace and harmony rather than despair and insanity. God is indeed using these experiences in many of our lives to cause us to be a human instrument to bring honor and glory to Him and to be bridge builders so that others will be able to go over the deep chasms of life. This reminds me of the poem "The Bridge Builder."

The Bridge Builder

An old man going a lone highway,
Came at the evening, cold and gray,
To a chasm vast and deep and wide

Through which was flowing a sullen tide;

The old man crossed in the twilight dim.

The sullen stream held no fears for him;

But he turned when safe on the other side

And built a bridge to span the tide.

"Old man," said a fellow pilgrim near,

You are wasting strength with building here,

Your journey will end with the ending day;

You never again will pass this way,

You have crossed the chasm deep and wide,

Why build you this bridge at the eventide?"

The builder lifted his old gray head,

"Good friend, in the path I have come," he said,

"There followeth after me today

A youth whose feet must pass this way.

This chasm that has been naught to me,

To that fair-haired youth may a pitfall be;

He, too, must cross in the twilight dim,

Good friend, I am building the bridge for him."

Will Allen Dromgoogle

(4) We must remember those that are behind us. None of us is an island unto ourselves. We are all being read and learned from by all men. Someone is watching us right now. Oh, to have it said, "He led me astray."

Isn't it a shame that there is so little concern for others today? Wouldn't you think that mothers and fathers would care enough for their own offspring that they would be willing to deny themselves their own lust and pleasures lest they hurt their own? Not only must we keep our eyes on Jesus, but we must understand that we are laying down a pattern for those coming behind us. We must build bridges so that those who are lame and hurting will find in their lives a bridge to victory and peace. Our condemnation will be not only what we have done or not done, nor what we have led others to do, but that we have bereaved those that are coming after us of the faith and hope they will need to fight their battle. I wonder how many men and women sitting in penal institutions today are there because they have merely followed their mom or dad or, perhaps, a friend, neighbor, or even a church member or a Christian. Remember, you have someone or ones following you—look around!

I plead with you, keep your eyes on Jesus by reading the blessed Bible each day. You can see Him even in types and patterns in the Old Testament and in the New Testament life and examples. Remember there are those who are watching you. We are all in the arena of life, perhaps being made a spectacle as were the Christians in Nero's day when he fed the Saints of God to the lions. Most importantly, there were millions of spectators then and now who have not been able to shake from their memory the victorious deaths, and the peace of God that was so evident on their faces. *"Yea, though we walk through the Valley of Death, we need not fear any evil, for He is with us,"* (Psalm 100).

It is with this intent that I have felt led of God to write this book. I do so with such a burden, lest any of us who truly want to be all that Jesus desires us to be might forget "This Way" that we are being led. I am deeply committed to the thought that God leads His dear people along–*some through great trials, some through the fire, but all through His blood*–that wherever He leads, He has the ultimate purpose of laying down a path for someone very close to you, so as to give them a pattern of good works.

In the coming chapters, I want to stir up your pure minds by way of remembrance concerning several areas where, if we do not keep them in mind, we will be rather a curse than a blessing, and rather than giving light we will obscure the path of life and peace.

May God bless you and give you a keen mind as we share our experiences and the experiences of others with the eventual purpose of keeping always in our mind that God works in mysterious ways, His wonders to perform.

Please remember that God is at work in this world through us to perform his perfect work of redemption. Once we are saved, we are to tell others.

The World's Bible

Christ has no hands but our hands

To do his work today;

He has no feet but our feet

To lead men in his way;

He has no tongue but our tongues

To tell men how he died;

He has no help but our help

To bring them to his side.

We are the only Bible

The careless world will read;

We are the sinner's gospel,

We are the scoffer's creed;

We are the Lord's last message,

Given in deed and word;

What if the type is crooked?

What if the print is blurred?

What if our hands are busy

With other work than his?

What if our feet are walking

Where sin's allurement is?

What if our tongues are speaking

Of things his lips would spurn?

How can we hope to help him

And hasten his return?

Annie Johnson Flint

Chapter 3
Seeing God in His sovereignty

Once again, let me remind you of the statement A.W. Pink made concerning this subject.

"It has often been pointed out that a fundamental requirement in expounding the word of God is a need of preserving the balance of truth. With this we are in hearty accord. Two things are beyond dispute: God is sovereign, man is responsible. ... There is real danger of overemphasizing the one and ignoring the other, we readily admit; and history furnishes numerous examples of both. To emphasize the sovereignty of God, without also maintaining the accountability of the creature, tends to fatalism; to be so concerned in maintaining the responsibility of man, as to lose sight of the sovereignty of God, is to exalt the creature and dishonor the creator."[5]

A.W. Pink

---

[5] Pink, A.W. The Sovereignty of God. The Banner of Truth Trust. London, Great Britian. 1928. P. 9

As we uncover the subject of sovereignty, let me be clear that this is not a doctrinal treatise but rather a layman's approach to a subject that I personally believe is beyond the comprehension of man. I remember reading a novel concerning a plantation slave in South Carolina, a deeply spiritual man who prayed about everything and said in writing to his friend, "I will come see you on Saturday night if God wills and the creek don't rise." It sort of goes along with the story about the men during the First World War when they said, "Praise the Lord and pass the ammunition." Dr. Irwin Lutzer, pastor of Moody Memorial Church, made this statement concerning understanding sovereignty in relationship to the Holocaust. He said, "In Ephesians 1:11, Paul reminds us 'That God works all things after the counsel of his will.'" Lutzer went on to say, "Regardless of your theological viewpoint on sovereignty, you will have to agree that even though the holocaust would not have happened if God had not chosen to permit it, figuratively speaking. He initiated the memo. He gave the green light. He did not do the evil but he chose to let evil happen."[6]

Napoleon, when asked which side he thought God was on, reflected and then said that it was probably the one with the largest Army. After the Battle of Waterloo, he said, "I guess man proposes, but it is God who disposes." In other words, he was saying, "It is God, not armies."

What a magnificent thought, that our God is sovereign! He is transcendent, meaning that God is overall, nothing goes beyond His notice, nor His permissive will. He is God!

---

[6] Lutzer, Irwin. Hitler's Cross. Moody Press, Chicago, Il 1995, p 51.

Our God reigns. Deuteronomy 33:27: *"The eternal God is thy refuge, and underneath are the everlasting arms, and he shall thrust out the enemy from before thee; and shall say: Destroy them."*

What we have noticed already is that these first-century Christians, as well as a host of others who have gone before us, were of a firm conviction that their commander—Jesus—had not only laid down a path or a pattern for them to walk in, but was as well working in their lives to cause them to be an example for others. They were convinced that Jesus was looking on. Bless your hearts, we must be of the same conviction! We must believe, as did they, that Jesus was not detached from them, but deeply involved in every facet of their lives, in the good times as well as in the bad times. In this chapter, I wish to show you how people, nations, and kings were helped, as it were, by the very hand of God. He controlled the all of it! For sure, there were times when the best of them doubted and concluded that all was lost, only to find out that at the last stroke of time, God stepped in.

One does not have to live very long before being confronted with events in this life that just do not add up or make any sense. We have all heard it said, or perhaps, have said ourselves that if there is a God in heaven, why would He allow such awful things to happen? In this chapter it certainly isn't my intention to try to explain all that we see or feel. There are many things in my own life that I don't have an answer to right now. However, it is my desire to show over and over again that God truly does work in mysterious ways, His wonders to perform. Behind all the events of history, in the building of nations and in the forming and transforming of men into the image of Christ, you can see the steady hand of God, shaping

39

and etching His desired will in mercy and in love. Ephesians 2:10: *"For we are his workmanship, created in Christ Jesus unto good works, which God hath before ordained that we should walk in them."*

A Sovereign God

What do we mean when we make this reference to God? Certainly, those who believe in God believe Him to be over all, knowing all, and being all-powerful. The theological terms for these definitions of God are omniscient, omnipotent, and omnipresent. We must believe in these sovereign characteristics or the God we serve would not be God.

However, there are extremely diverging opinions when it comes to this subject. I guess we have all heard silly arguments, such as: *"Could God make a rock that He could not pick up?"* or, *"If God is all powerful, why does He allow evil, which He is to hate?"* or *"If God is love, why does He allow unloving things to happen?"* Really, it is in these very simple thoughts that a lot of controversy arises and also much confusion, misunderstanding and even bitterness.

First Cause

One position is: God is the first cause. By that we mean that theologians and people purposed that God started or instigated this whole cosmic system. Then, after the initial generation, God sat back and is watching it run down. One philosopher called this "The Big Clock Theory." This theory makes God a very impersonal God and even at times calloused, indifferent, and even insensitive to His creation. Things are pretty much left up to random change and random chance. Things are just happening.

Cause and Effect–Fatalism or Fate Clause

This can be referred to as a hyper or extreme position on the side of God. People who are proponents of this position hold to the basic theory that William Shakespeare advocated when he was suffering the loss of a dear friend. He said that life is a stage and we humans are mere actors dangling on strings as puppets. You can see and even almost feel the fatalism and the lamentation in his voice as he looks at the dreadful experience he is going through and can only conclude that if there is a God, He is just manipulating us, and almost—if not altogether—enjoying it.

Several years ago, a friend of our family was struggling through some very difficult times. It seemed as if her whole world was falling apart. Her father, who was a farmer and a very fine Christian man, just lost his poultry in a snowstorm. Shortly after the storm, he had a heart attack and was not able to provide for his family. This is a good Christian family but in those emotional moments their thoughts were, "Why is God allowing this?" In her frustration and hurt, our friend said, "Perhaps God enjoys seeing us squirm." Well, thank God, she didn't stay in that hurt very long. She was able to work her way through the suffering to help and comfort.

These are the *inexplicables* and, humanly speaking, there appear to be no answers. Because of it, many turn to this extreme position of sovereignty. They conclude that God is over all and that everything that happens is ordained by God and is irrevocable. Therefore, we must just suffer.

Through it, after all, we are mere puppets on God's omnipotent string. This is just our fate.

Do you remember reading in the book of Ecclesiastes how King Solomon had backslidden and was interpreting everything from a purely humanist position. He said, concerning man in Ecclesiastes 3:18-19, *"I said in mine heart concerning the estate of the sons of men, that God might manifest them, and that they might see that they themselves are beasts? For that which befalleth the sons of men befalleth beasts; even one thing befalleth them: as the one dieth, so dieth the other, yea, they have all one breath; so that a man hath no preeminence above a beast: for all is vanity."*

I guess you have even heard the ridiculous statement about the man who fell down the steps. At the bottom, he got up, shook himself off and said, "I am glad that is over." Meaning that God has every little detail of life laid down and everything that happens, even falling down, was in the foreknowledge of God. How absurd! Perhaps, if he had been careful, he could have avoided such a tumble.

Yes, God is certainly sovereign and does, in fact, know everything and works in the events of life to shape and change individuals and nations. However, we conclude that men ultimately have a free choice. In another chapter we will discuss the matter as it relates itself to prayer. If, in fact, everything is so settled, why pray? Does prayer change things? Can we pray and change the mind and heart of God? Please stay with me, as I am going to discuss these questions a little later on. We will take Biblical principles and examples to show how much man is involved in the affairs of people and national events.

Now, by the grace of God, let me show you what I believe the Bible teaches. Allow us to refer to our position as *Cause and Response*–we refer to this as God's Ultimate.

Some hold to an extreme position of God's sovereignty to the exclusion of man's influence in anything. In theological circles this is called *Superlapsarianism*. There are others who have a less extreme position on sovereignty and that is *lapsarianism*. This is the idea that while they understand sovereignty, at the same time they see man's involvement in the overall scheme of things. However, just like every other doctrine in the Bible, there are two sides: God's commands and man's responsibility. I am sorry, but that is just the way it is. Although behind the thinking and working of man is the strong voice of God, man can refuse to listen and become stubborn in his ways and ultimately frustrate even the grace of God. So, somewhere between the sovereign plan and pattern of God, there is the human involvement at work, and I might add that this is very intrinsically needed.

Now, as we refer to this as *Cause and Response*, we do so because we believe that behind the sovereign working of God, He has a specific and desired will to perform. We thus refer to it as God's Ultimate. What do we mean by that? Well, allow me to use a very familiar story taken from the Bible. The story I refer to is the massive exodus of 600,000 people of God, people from the land of Egypt, to the wonderful Promised Land. As we look at this story, there are some things that immediately capture our attention and cause us to ponder. Why would God choose the route that he did when leading His people out? Certainly, we all have experienced,

43

even in our own lifetime, things and events that just do not add up or make sense. It is in these events that some of God's people lose heart, and thus lose faith, and eventually lose hope. Rather than becoming blessed Christians, they become angry, defeated souls. Remember how we stated in our introduction, that those first-century Christians held on to God and found solace in His leading and words of comfort.

Well, the people of this mass exodus were faced with the same dilemma. What is God all about? Does he know what He is doing? Now, I think we begin to really appreciate Moses at this point. After all, the people could not see God; they could only see Moses. They did not meet with God as Moses did. They did not hear the voice of God, the clear leading of God, or the specific plan as Moses did. Therefore, when things went wrong, their blame towards God was transferred to Moses, and all their rebellion was directed towards him. You know, it is just like that today. God's men surely need our prayers because, most often, they only have the basic plan before them and do not know all the ways God in His sovereignty will work. We must, as Israel did, come back to God and ask for wisdom and patience to see our faith step through to completion.

In the midst of all their questions, God gave them insight as to the "why" of the Wilderness of Zin. As the exiting Hebrews left the capitol city of Ramses, the normal way would be to travel out toward the west to the coast of the Mediterranean Sea. From there they could have followed the coastline up toward Beersheba into Jerusalem. This was the caravan route and was well traveled. On this route there was much sustenance and water supplies. After all, everyone went this way, and it was thought by all to be the only logical path. It was also the shortest and the journey could be accomplished in a mere 8-10 days. It was also the safest. However, this was not God's choosing. We get a glimpse into the "why" of God's leading in Exodus 13:17:

"And it came to pass, when Pharaoh had let the people go, that God led them not through the way of the land of the Philistines, although that was near; God said, 'Lest the people repent when they see war, and they return to Egypt.'" This verse basically states that although God knew the short way was the most logical, He also knew something else. Because when God makes a decision, He not only makes it based on the past and present but, because He is sovereign, He can also look into the future. In His glimpse into the future, He realized that if He were to lead them up along the coast, they would have been defeated, because the coastal route led through Beersheba, which was the land of the Philistines. Israel had been in slavery for forty years. They had learned much concerning farming and common labor, but they knew nothing of war.

Now, to gain further insight into God's choice, we need to turn to Deuteronomy 8:2: *"And thou shalt remember all the way which the Lord thy God led thee these forty years in the wilderness, to humble thee and to test thee, to know what was in thine heart, whether thou wouldest keep his commandments, or not."*

Here I believe, we get a more complete picture of God's leading. In verse 2, we notice God's ultimate desire for the people was two-fold.

(1) He wanted them to know Him more intimately. In Egypt, because of their long exile, a new generation had been born who did not know

Jehovah. They knew much of the Pharaoh and the Egyptians, but they had lost their own identity and their relationship to God. You see, the way of God's choosing demanded that their faith be renewed, stretched, and challenged. It was in this leading that God could once again prove to His people His ability to supply all their needs and work His wonders to perform. It was here in the wilderness that these dear people would be totally dependent on Him. Here is where the miracles were needed and only God's provision would sustain them.

(2) The second reason for God choosing this route was because He wanted His people to know themselves. He wanted them to know their limitations; He wanted them to know their temptations; and most of all, He wanted them to be fully cognizant of their potential. They would never have learned this had they not been placed at the very door of man's total inability. They would never have learned how, by just obeying God's command, they could capture a walled city that was thought by many to be absolutely impregnable. The crossing of the Red Sea, and later the crossing of the Jordan, were both marvelous experiences and testimonies of God's provision.

Now, had the children of Israel given into their fears and anxieties and returned to the bondage of Egypt, they would never have had the glorious experiences that they did with God.

You see, God's ultimate desire was to have the proper response from the people He so dearly loved. So, when we talk of sovereignty, we are not talking about a powerful, insensitive God—one who likes to see us squirm—but a very personal God. Our God is a very intimate God and a very loving God who only intends to work so as to cause us to come to know him better and ultimately to cause us to be a living epistle, learned and read of all men.

Yes, God is the Ultimate Cause behind everything–from the first act of Creation until this very moment. We must also believe that not even a sparrow falls to the ground without Him noticing, because all His ways have a divine cause meant to produce a proper response.

Now, let us trace this sovereign God in the making of nations, noticing that with each cause He was deepening a people to respond in such a way that we who came behind might see and be encouraged.

God at Work in Nations

A few years ago I had the distinct privilege of traveling to Colorado and eventually into Colorado Springs where Pikes Peak is found. As we descended back into Colorado Springs we saw, to our right, wagon wheel tracks that had been imprinted into the meadow. The tour guide told us that those tracks were made over 100 years ago by the wagon that carried the author of America the Beautiful. She was an English teacher at the University of Colorado. As they ascended this magnificent peak and she was able to gaze out at the beautiful vista, being able to see at least three states, and she wrote the lyrics to that wonderful song. "America, America, God shed His grace on thee, and crowned thy good with brotherhood from sea to shining sea." I have recently been intrigued by a book called, *The Light and The Glory*, by Peter Marshall and David Manuel. The purpose for their writing this book came about through a discussion they had in which the question arose as to whether God was really behind the discovery of America and if, in fact, the Bible was the foundation from which the early fathers gleaned their background for the framing of the Constitution and the article bylaws. What was amazing to the authors was that as they set out to do their research, they found virtually no evidence whatsoever to substantiate that God was, in fact, in the overall founding of this great nation. Though they were convinced that God was in it, where could they find the evidence? You see, from the late eighteen hundreds, most of the historians were very liberal in their religion and were biased in their presentation of history.

It was through prayer and much hard work that they began to uncover the evidence they prayerfully believed to be there. It was not until they went down into the cellars of the great libraries of Harvard, Yale, Princeton, and the Library of Congress that they began to find golden nuggets on dusty shelves that for the most part had been forgotten and, in most recent cases, had never been told. It was here they found facts about Christopher Columbus, whose name literally means Christ-bearer. He was not a bigot whose only ambition was to find gold(as liberal historians would like us to believe) but he had, in fact, been convinced that God was calling him to literally fulfill His plan of reaching the ends of the world with the gospel of Christ. A verse of scripture that he felt God had given to him specifically is found in Isaiah 49:1-6:

> "Listen, o coasts, unto me; and hearken, ye peoples, from
> far: The Lord hath called me from the womb; from the
> body of my mother hath He made mention of my name.

And He hath made my mouth like a sharp sword; in the
shadow of his hand hath He hidden me, and made me a
polished shaft; in His quiver hath He hidden me. And said
unto me, Thou art my servant, O Israel, in whom I will be
glorified. Then I said, I have labored in vain, I have spent
my strength for nothing, and in vain, yet surely the justice
due to me is with the Lord, and my work with my God.
And now, said the Lord who formed me from the womb
to be His servant, to bring Jacob again to Him, Though
Israel be not gathered, yet shall I be glorious in the eyes
of the Lord, and my God shall be my strength. And He
said, It is a light thing that thou shouldest be my servant
to raise up the tribes of Jacob, and to restore the preserved
of Israel; I will also give thee for a light to the nations, that
thou mayest be my salvation unto the end of the earth."

It is hard to say where the idea of his mission had crystallized. It may
have been while he was a teenage boy in Genoa carding wool in his family's wool shop, as his father and grandfather had done before him. Or
perhaps it was in 1484 in Lisbon, the sea-faring capitol of the world, where
he was employed with his brother Bartholomew in the select profession
of mapmaking. He would have been 33 years old at that time. It was in his
astute studies that he came to the conclusion that if he traversed the 28th
parallel, the distance from the Canary Islands to Cipangu was only 750
leagues, or approximately 2,760 miles. You see, it was God already behind
the undertaking, and where God guides you, He supplies you with all you

need. The remarkable discovery was that, yes, in fact God was at the very core of the discovery of this great land here in the Western Hemisphere.

Now, just because you are in the providential will of God, it does not mean that you will have an easy time or even a blessed time. It seems as though, just as God had more in mind for Israel than Canaan, He also had more in mind for Columbus than the West Indies. Columbus had a free will and at times was of a rebellious nature. He, like many of us, seemed to be the closest to God when things were not going so well. However, when events in his life were filled with the good pleasures of life, Columbus became full of pride and very carnal. During these self-willed occasions, God would let the hammer of divine providence fall on him to break his pride and once again get his attention.

Not only in the early years of our country, but throughout our history, it is so interesting to notice the small events that seemed to shape the entire course of our nation, and even cause it to survive. Many historians believe that had not Adolf Hitler become so obsessed with power, he could have, perhaps, won the War of the Century. There was one major flaw in his make up–he hated the Jews and put his hatred in vengeance against them. He did not realize that he was, in essence, putting his heart against God. Though he had, perhaps, the best and most gifted scientists of his day, because he put his hand against God's people, he caused the arm of God to come against him.

The same is true with individuals. Throughout history, it was God at work behind the scenes.

Napoleon, who was raised an agnostic and then became an atheist, came to know Christ later in life. It is said that one man who knew Christ visited Napoleon and kept asking him the same question: "Why it was that Jesus Christ accomplished more through peace than Alexander the Great and you together could accomplish through war?" It is said that these thoughts so occupied his heart and mind that one evening when he was weary with this agonizing question, he fell on his knees and said, "Jesus, I surrender." You can understand a military man saying that. Praise God, behind this proud man, there was the small voice of God at work!

I have also been intrigued with how God worked in Israel's day. Do you remember in II Kings 6 when Elisha was in Dothan and the Syrians came to take him? They were angry with him because he would tell their secrets, and King Ben-hadad was accusing the soldiers of betraying confidences and revealing battle strategies. One of the King's aides suggested that perhaps the information was being leaked because God was giving that secret information to His prophet Elisha, who was becoming well known throughout the whole kingdom. So Ben-hadad sent a great host of warriors to find the prophet kill him and do away with this menace. So they came in great array, and when the servant of Elisha saw the great hosts, he was so afraid that he cried out to this man of God and said, *"What shall we do?"* Then the Bible says that Elisha prayed to God and said, *"Lord, I pray thee, open his eyes that he may see."* When he could see properly, he saw the hosts of heaven standing all around. That day God, wrought a magnificent victory without even shedding a drop of blood.

51

I wonder how many times God wishes we could see as we should. Though at times it looks as though there is no hope, our sovereign God can and will intervene at just the right time. Perhaps this is the assurance that Job had when he said, "Though he slay me, yet will I trust Him."

A good friend of mine went to see his mother who was dying. When he arrived he found her sore troubled and sobbing into her pillow. She was suffering from a beginning state of dementia. He asked, "Momma why are you so troubled?" and she said, "I am afraid to die." He said, "Momma can't we trust Jesus?" At that moment, she stopped crying. As with individuals, as well as nations we must understand that behind the visible world, there is the unseen hand of God at work.

When the Puritans first came to this country in 1620, they had experienced what few people in this present world could begin to understand or imagine. They had left their native land because of the religious persecution to which they were submitted. One of them was a young man by the name of William Bradford. Bradford was a man of about 29 years of age and very pious. He, along with 86 others, had left England because of the persecution they were receiving from the Church of England, presided over by the House of Bishops. The church hierarchy had grown increasingly alarmed at the growth of two movements of fanatics. The first and by far larger group claimed to be dedicated to "purifying the church from within." The Puritans, as they were sarcastically dubbed, were growing more and more in disfavor with the church.

The second group, which the Bishops considered more dangerous, were those who believed the Church was already corrupt beyond any possibility of purification. They chose to separate themselves from it and conduct their own worship. They were also sarcastically given a name, the Separatists. These people were hounded, bullied, and forced to pay assessments to the church. Many of them were thrown into prison on trumped-up charges or driven underground. They met in private homes and were in constant fear for their very lives.

There were, of course, those who came to the new continent for only one reason–the love of gold and fortune. Certainly, these people were the ones who would never adjust to the many trials and difficulties that they would have to endure in order to succeed. You see, unless you have a cause in life that is bigger than yourself, you will soon lose interest. The other two groups were men and woman who deeply felt that their voyage to this new land was indeed a missionary journey. They were inspired every bit as was the Apostle Paul.

The voyage across that Atlantic was so long and difficult that to this day journals have been written and navigational logs still record how fierce the North Atlantic can become. The dear people, almost as soon as they had left the fair shores of Holland, were met with a relentless winter storm. A small ship called the Mayflower was all but torn apart by the constant gales, which endured for four months. Because of this enormous, tempestuous sea, the inhabitants were not allowed to go top-side for even a breath of fresh air. The crew became so sick and malnourished that it appeared after a while that none of them would survive. In fact, the sickness became so awful that the stench caused even the ship's captain to begin to pray for God to be merciful and allow them all to die. One of the crew members laughed at the God-fearing people and mocked the God to whom he saw them praying. One day he stood up and said mockingly, "You will all be fed to the fish long before this ship reaches the New England shore." As God would have it, the only one to be fed to the fish was this ill-kept, foul wretch who, though he placed his hand against God's people, gained nothing from it. What a lesson we should all learn from the stories of not only these people, but to all people around the world who are God's people.

The day finally came when God in his mercy had finally allowed the battered ship with this priceless cargo to arrive on the shores of New England, the place where His sovereign will was to be accomplished. God was sifting a nation, that He might send choice grain into the wilderness.

William Bradford stood on the deck of the Mayflower that cold, snowy, wintry day on December 6th, and along with his tiny army gave thanks and went on record to the fact that only God could have seen them through this voyage. He then took a small boat to shore with six other men. The wind and the snow almost cut them to shreds. When they finally landed, there was nothing to welcome them but snowdrifts and solid tundra from which, once again, God would build a foundation which stands even to this day. We must never forget the enormous price that was paid. Of the 88 on board, half of them had died that first winter due to the environment, and lack of shelter and food. Time does not permit me now to go into the details of that first winter, but I can only ask myself how any human could endure such a ravishing ordeal. The only conclusion I can come to is that they were guided by deep convictions and principles. Those who came for gold and fortune were the first to die, some by suicide. However, these "fanatics," as they were called back in the motherland, were convinced that God was teaching them to die to self and live for Him and each other. Historians, even to this day, give this record, and some even say that the main reason that this New England colony survived and the others didn't, such as the Jamestown Colony, was because they lived for each other. You see, the Jamestown Colony was founded on the misnomer that the entire landmass in Virginia was resting on a gold mine, which was later proven to be fool's gold. The Massachusetts Bay Colony, as it was later called, was God's miracle. Yes, He did allow it to be sifted, and it appeared to be almost destroyed, but He was preparing it for a wonderful harvest. John 12:24, *"Verily, verily, I say unto you, Except a grain of wheat fall into the ground and die, it abideth alone; but if it die, it bringeth forth much fruit."*

When he returned to the ship after having surveyed the land that he was convinced could only sustain them if God would permit and if the people were committed, William Bradford was faced with the news that while he was gone his wife had jumped overboard and had drowned. How much could any one man take? Where was God? Why would God cause the North Atlantic gales to be so relentless and fierce? Was there no compassion on His part? Could God not see that these dear people and this man of God were already on the very edge of defeat? How could He do this?

In this chapter I have just wanted to state in a very simple way, that if we are to finish our course with "joy," we must have a deep conviction of the sovereignty of our God. He does at times seem to move contrary to human understanding. He does cause the seed in His time to die that it might grow, and, as we have already stated in regards to Israel in the wilderness, His ultimate purpose was not for them to simply enter into the land of Canaan, but that they truly learn of Him and completely understand themselves. This is what God is all about. In fact, that is what the whole Bible is about. Though there is a scarlet thread of redemption that winds itself through the Scripture from Genesis to the Book of Revelation, there is so much more. Truly God desired and planned after the fall of Adam for His people to come back into fellowship with Him. He also has a deeper purpose.

The Puritans were convinced before they left the shore of Leyden, Holland, that they had entered into a covenant with God. Thus, they called themselves "The New Israel." They believed, just as Abraham did, that they had entered into a contract with God, and if they would live up to their end of the bargain, God would ultimately fulfill His end.

Beloved, you and I must believe the same if we ever hope to be more than conquerors. We must see the promises of God, and then do our best to meet the conditions of such a promise. There is a song that is popular these days, which says, "When you can't see His hand, trust His heart." Dear friend, when you can't understand His ways, trust His heart. We must trust His heart, when we can't see His hand. Trust Him, only trust Him!

Chapter 4
Seeing God in our suffering

"We must through much tribulation enter into the kingdom of God."

Acts 14:22

"Yet man is born unto trouble, as the sparks fly upward."

Job 5:7

About a year ago, I was invited to the home of a friend of mine. He was dying with leukemia and I was asked to come because the family had been warned by their doctor that it was a matter of a few days before he would pass away. When I arrived at the house, I was not prepared for what I was about to see. I did not recognize the man lying there before me. The man that I knew was a tremendous athlete. Jim was in his late 40's and had the physique of a much younger man. Now cancer had reduced him to a mere shell of a man. I tried very hard not to show the shock that I was experiencing. He reached out his hand and tried to grasp mine, but he was too weak to even shake my hand. He had been incoherent, but today he was aware of his surroundings and somehow I believe that it was God who allowed this final meeting between him and me. I remember when I preached in his church, Jim would give a hearty "Amen," and then come up and thank me for my message. We played many a golf game together and I so envied his ability to hit the golf ball consistently over 300 yards. He said, "Brother Dave, I need to tell you of something that just happened to me yesterday that has given me the comfort that I have been so desperately searching for." Then he told me this story.

"About five years ago, I had attended a Bible Conference where one of the preachers emphasized the need to be conscious of the souls that are around us." He then said, "As I was traveling back from the conference, the Holy Spirit seemed to tell me to go to my pastor and tell him that I wanted to start a visiting program whereby we would go into houses all around our church." Before long, he found himself before the pastor sharing his heart and his burden. The pastor was much encouraged by his burden and said that they would set aside a day every week to visit people. The pastor would go down one street and Jim would go down another.

"On the very first visit," Jim said, "I had not gone far until I knocked on the door. A young man opened it to see what I wanted. Brother Dave, that day I led that man to Christ and I have not seen him nor heard of him since. The other day, however, a knock came to my door and my wife went to answer it. A UPS delivery man said, 'I have a package for Jim Devine. Is this where he lives?'"

The wife acknowledged that he had the right address. The UPS man then said, "Is this the Jim Devine that lived on a certain street in Erie, PA?" His wife said, "Yes it is." He asked, "Is Jim here?" When she said yes, he asked if he could see him. Jim's wife informed him that Jim was dying and unable to have visitors. The UPS man said, "I must see him. You see, Jim led me to Christ five years ago and I would like to thank him." Carol asked Jim if he was up to having a visitor. Jim said yes. The young man came into the room and knelt by the bed of my friend and said, "Jim, you probably do not remember me, but that evening when you came to my house, my wife had left and I was loading a .357 magnum to take my life. You intervened and led me to Christ and now I too am doing what you did for me, telling other people about the Lord."

After telling the story, Jim looked at me and said, "Dave, so often I have felt like our labor was in vain when we went door to door, but now I realize how God indeed used me. You see Dave, its okay for me to die now because now I have a young Timothy who is coming after me. God does everything right!"

A week later, Jim went home to be with his Lord.

I have heard people argue that tribulation does not make a man, but tribulation reveals a man. I personally beg to differ with that, because I believe that in our trials we are shaped and molded by God as you will see in this chapter. One old Puritan writer once said, "We never know ourselves till we are thoroughly tried." Then he used the illustration of a ship. He said, "Marines speak of a ship finding herself." The only way in which a ship can find herself is by launching out into the deep and encountering the storm, the whirlwind and the gale. Man finds himself in tribulation. Fear is a language God understands.

"He washed my eyes with tears that I might see."

Though most of us would want to shun the tribulations and heartaches of life, most of us would conclude—as did the songwriter of the above lyrics—that it is, in fact, in these times that we not only find ourselves, but we also find God in a deeper way.

Whenever we think of suffering, those who know the Bible usually think immediately of Job. We remember that he was a good man and one who feared God and hated sin. However, it was this man who God allowed to come under the attack of the devil. Which of us has not been moved to read with great consternation the awful tragedies that came upon this man? Which of us did not say, at least within ourselves, "How could he bear up underneath it all?" Then we stand absolutely amazed as we hear him conclude in Job 13:15, *"Though he slay me, yet will I trust in Him; but I will defend mine own ways before Him."*

Those of you who know me, or have heard me speak, have also heard me sing. You know that one of my favorite songs is, *O, Rejoice in the Lord*, written by Ron Hamilton. The song was based on the text taken from Job 23:10, *"But He knoweth the way that I take; when He hath tested me, I shall come forth as gold."*

Ron Hamilton was in the hospital awaiting eye surgery. He was told that, perhaps, when he awoke from the surgery, he would be blind. Ron gives testimony that as he lay on his bed that night, he had many thoughts going through his mind, but he sensed the peace of God. The verse in Job came to mind, and he wrote a song. The first stanza goes like this:

"God never moves without purpose or plan when he's trying his

servants and molding his man,

O, give thanks to the Lord though your testings seem long, in dark-

ness He giveth a song.

60

O, Rejoice in the Lord, for He makes no mistakes, He knoweth the

end of each path that I take,

and when I am tried and purified, I shall come forth as gold."

As we continue to walk this pilgrimage, we must not only understand and be convinced that there is a sovereign God looking on, but that He also personally gets involved in our lives to make us better. I often refer to Ephesians 2:10, *"For we are his workmanship, created in Christ Jesus unto good works, which God hath before ordained that we should walk in them."* What Paul is saying in this verse is that God is the master potter, we are on the wheel of His omnipotence, and He is still working, molding and framing us to ultimately become what He has in mind for us.

Because God made us in the first place, He knows what it is that we need and how much we can endure. Our best has always been His desire, from the very outset. God knows how much wind and rain to send, and how many storms we can endure. He does not want to break us, but only to mold us into His pattern.

In this chapter we are going to talk about suffering and how it relates to our walk and the will of God.

Why do the godly suffer?

A number of years ago a friend of mine said to me, "Dave, over the title of the book of James I wrote this inscription: *A Missouri Church.*" Then he said, "What is it that the people of Missouri are known for?" I replied, "Well, I guess everyone knows that this state is referred to as the *Show Me*

State. They even say so on their license plates. In other words, they are the kind of people who say, 'I have heard what you say, now show me!'"

You know, I think we are all like this. Most of us have heard some pretty good sermons and have heard some men wax eloquent, only to find out that what they say and what they do are not always the same. I don't know about you, but I am longing to see some men that can not only talk it, but walk it as well.

As I study the book of James, that is exactly what I believe Pastor James had in mind when he wrote this letter, or perhaps, first of all *spoke* this letter to his church. He wanted them to have an impact on the entire city of Jerusalem, and he knew the only way would be for them to live what they were preaching. You remember that this was exactly what Jesus said when He gave His famous sermon on the mount. He told the disciples in Matthew 4:16, *"Let your light so shine before men, that they may see your good works, and glorify your Father, who is in heaven."* Jesus knew only too well that most sermons which are caught are taught by an obedient and careful walk. As I thought about this statement concerning the book of James, I asked myself, "What was it about this book that caused my friend to call it the *Missouri Book* or the *Show Me Book?*" Allow me to tell you how God directed me.

One day as I was reading through my Bible, I came upon a passage that caused me to stop, think, and gain some light on the subject at hand. It might appear at first to be a bit obscure but if you bear with me, I think I will make my point.

The passage is in Acts 12:5. It reads as follows: *"Peter, therefore, was kept in prison; but prayer was made without ceasing by the church unto God for him."* Here is what caught my attention about this verse. You see, persecution was beginning to come to the church in Jerusalem. After the resurrection, Pastor James—the half brother of Jesus—went back to the City of Jerusalem, and because of the fire in his bosom he began to tell his story about the risen Christ. It was not long before great numbers of people hearing the story believed it, and repented. As is usually the case, the devil soon raised up an adversary against these new Christians by way of the Roman authority in that part of the world, Herod. This Herod (of which there were several), was the grandson of King Herod who, when he heard the Messiah was born, had all the babies two years old and under put to death. Joseph and Mary, however, took Jesus and went to Egypt. This Herod, also fearing what he was hearing, decided to put such fear into the believers that they would cease their activities. He took one of their members, also called James, and had him beheaded. Now, my question is this: What was it about these people that caused them to keep on believing and praying? Would you and I be like this? Would your church be like this? In other words, would we believe in prayer if it appeared that God hadn't answered our prayer? Don't you think the church must have prayed in earnest for the safety of their friend James? Don't you suspect that they must have pleaded for God to deliver him? Yet, he was martyred before the entire city.

Now, on the footfalls of the martyrdom of James, Peter comes into town. Herod, seeing how he had already pleased the crowd with his vengeance against James, proceeded further to promote his notoriety by taking Peter. However, because it was the Passover and all Jews were involved with their religious festivities, he put him in jail, intending to bring him forth and kill him after Easter, and perhaps, put this matter to rest once and for all.

Also, what so arrested my attention was the wording of verse 5: *"Prayer was made without ceasing by the church unto God for him."* What was it about these people that caused them to still believe God? After all, they had already prayed for one of their members, and God did not answer that prayer, at least as far as they could see. Was God showing partiality? Did He love Peter more than James? Was Peter more important than James? What was it about these early believers to make them call for yet another meeting and not only pray, but pray without ceasing? My goodness, would we be like that? Would your church be like that? Would you have made it to that prayer meeting, or would you have made some excuse as to why you were too busy, the reason really being that you had now lost confidence in prayer? Would you now have seeds of doubts beginning to root in your soul, taking a toll on your spiritual desires?

Well, they did pray, and God in his sovereignty and mercy set Peter free! How I love to read that story over and over again. I come away encouraged. My point is, what was it about this church and these believers that kept them praying even when it seemed as though God didn't answer their prayers and reward the efforts of their previous meeting? I think the answer can be found in the book of James. Take notice of what it was that this Pastor, James, built within his people to cause them to have such a solid faith and unwavering confidence in God.

Now, wouldn't you agree that most of us are looking for someone to come along and not only talk about how we should be willing to suffer but demonstrate it as well? Also, in this business of serving, isn't it refreshing to find people who not only talk about loving Jesus but demonstrate it by their willingness to roll up their sleeves and put feet to their faith?

We are also very unimpressed when we hear someone who is supposed to be a good Christian using his tongue as fire to destroy and cause great harm to the body of Christ. When it comes to the secret life, we must all be so careful. Most of us, if not all of us, are guilty in this area. We all have secret sins that are personal to us, and we would never want them to be known. However, I believe God knows them, and because He knows them, we are not as productive as we could be. Now, once again, I am not suggesting that anyone is perfect, but we must be willing to confess our sins to God, and He is willing to forgive us and cleanse us from all ungodliness. Our secret life, oh, my, how often I have seen it manifested. You see, Jesus said that if we are not careful He would shout it from the housetops or the birds of the air would carry it. Oh, may God help us!

The Bible also declares that there is coming a day when the counsels of the heart shall be declared. My friend, we must strive after holiness without which no man shall see God.

The fifth chapter of James deals with the Christian in relationship to the Second Coming. The pastor concludes his admonition by stating that all these areas of life should be tempered with the fact that Jesus is coming again! Hallelujah! What a day of rejoicing that is going to be! In fact, Pastor James told his people that they were to practice patience. *"Be patient therefore, brethren, unto the coming of the Lord,"* (James 5:7). In all things we must have patience; we are not home yet.

Some other verses in the scriptures that have caused me to take hope in my trials are: *"For I reckon that the sufferings of this present time are not worthy to be compared with the glory which shall be revealed in us,"* (Romans 8:18). *"For ye have need of patience, that, after ye have done the will of God, ye might receive the promise,"* (Hebrews 10:36). Paul seems to bring all things into proper focus when he so boldly declares in Romans 8:38-39, *"For I am persuaded, that neither death, nor life, nor angels, nor principalities, nor powers nor things present, nor things to come, Nor height, nor depth, nor any other creature, shall be able to separate us from the love of God, which is in Christ Jesus our Lord."*

Certainly, my friends, we have so much in Christ. As we have taken a quick overlook of this book, we can already see what an outstanding job this pastor did in covering all the bases with his people so as to prepare them for the work that was ahead of them. Before we leave it, I want to go back and zero in on the first chapter.

You remember that this chapter refers to the Christian in relationship to his suffering. Now, if there is any one place that will put our faith to the test, it is in this area of suffering, especially when it comes home to us. It is here that we will have such a temptation to doubt, and even give in to our despair and become a spiritual casualty. It is also here, I am deeply convinced, where God has our most dynamic and most persuasive argument on behalf of God's power and love to demonstrate to the world that He can and is willing to work though it with us. It is here in the awful valley of despair and heartache where the Lily of the Valley comes with the beauty and fragrance of heaven to be our strength and to bear our grief. It is here where others take notice and many begin, perhaps, for the first time to hear our message. For you see, it is here they can identify with us. It is here where *your* sufferings can be compared to *their* sufferings. It is here where hope can once again take wings in their soul and put their fear, doubts, bitterness, and heartaches to rest once and for all.

If we Christians never had trouble, burdens or heartaches, how could we ever hope to understand and give counsel to the many who do? If we never knew a time when we needed mercy and grace, how could we tell others who are in such need? God's grace is sufficient. We would be mere hypocrites. We would tend to become as the Pharisees. You see, the main problem with the Pharisees was they condemned and made others do things, such as causing them to carry grievous burdens, about which they themselves knew nothing.

That is the reason we have all heard many times that someone referring to someone else as a Pharisee. The term "hypocrites" come to mind as well. Both of these labels describe a person who thought he had all the answers and was full of advice. However, when done speaking, words fall on deaf ears. The reason being he knew not of what he spoke. You and I would agree that these people have nothing to give. On the other hand, when we meet a person who has walked where we are walking, we latch on to every word he says. When he is speaking, it feels as though it is God speaking and we are transfixed by his every word. So, I guess if we truly want a ministry of helps, we must be willing to allow God to develop us for such a task.

Concerning Jesus, the Bible says in Hebrews 4:15, *"For we have not an high priest which cannot be touched with the feeling of our infirmities; but was in all points tempted like as we are, yet without sin."* Jesus understands us because He sat where we sit, He walked where we are walking, and He hurt like many of us are hurting. You remember in the beginning of this book, we established the fact that we can never go anywhere in this world, or have any experiences that He has not first of all gone through beforehand to give us a perfect example.

Many of us expect Him to be triumphant and victorious, but it is quite another thing when we see one of our contemporaries, one of our own, being just as adequate and just as victorious. It is this present example that God is using to once again lay down a pattern so that our friends, relatives, and contemporaries can have a beautiful example to encourage them in their walk, and for all the others who come after them, to help them find hope and help even in the midst of their hurting. They have seen you.

Just yesterday, I was told a story that I shall never forget and I feel constrained by God to tell it to you as best I can remember. I came to an area to preach a revival meeting. After the Sunday morning service, the pastor, his wife, and their married son, Jerry, took me out for dinner. On the way back to the farm retreat, where I would be staying for the week, Jerry told me this story.

He said, "Dave, this is a tough time of the year for me. You see, it was two years ago tomorrow that my four-year old son died. He had cerebral palsy, and my dear wife had to force-feed him on many occasions. He was getting weaker all the time, and he had no control over his body." With tears streaming down his face, he told me how on the morning his son died, he did not go in to kiss him goodbye as he usually did before leaving the house for work. While on the job that morning he was called home, only being told there was a problem. When he reached his home, his son was gone. He went along in the ambulance with his wife and son to the hospital.

He said, "Dave, seeing my son lying there was so hard on us. We have never felt so bad in all of our lives." He then told me that as he was leaving the hospital, he looked through the windshield of his car, and saw before him the clouds separating and there, in the middle, were a vast number of children playing. He said, "Dave, there were thousands of them," and then back in the crowd came this little boy running up to him. It was *his* boy. He said, "Daddy don't worry, I am happy now, and I am waiting for you and Mommy." Then he added, "I felt so much peace." He said to his wife, "Did you see that?"

"See what?" she asked.

Jerry said, "I knew she might not understand right then, but I did tell her later."

How my heart was touched as this young man told me his heartache. Just across the room from where I am sitting is a picture of Jerry's son. You see, where I am staying this week is a retreat. No one lives here. It is used as a place of refuge and a place to retreat. I wonder how many times Jerry slips away up here in the mountains, just to spend time with his thoughts.

Jerry then said, "Dave, I have another heartache. I have a little two-year old daughter. Because of a reaction to a shot when she was just an infant, she now goes into seizures every day, and the doctors say she could go into heart failure and die anytime." Don't you wonder why some seem to have so much to carry? Isn't it only natural to look up into the face of heaven and ask, "God, why?" Certainly, it is. That is why James, in the first chapter and in verse five, encouraged his people to do just that. He said, *"If any of you lack wisdom, let him ask of God, that giveth to all men liberally, and upbradeth not; and it shall be given him."* You see, God does not want us to be spiritual ignoramuses. He wants us to know. The word *wisdom* in this verse means God's perspective or God's point of view. He wants us to know why He is working. It is also interesting to see that God makes it very clear in this verse, that He does not hold it against us, nor is He offended when we come with the question, "Why?"

I have heard so many say that we are not supposed to ask, "Why?" They even go so far as to say it is sin. Nonsense! In this chapter on suffering, James is making it very clear that we can and we should come to our Father for wisdom!

It was for experiences such as this that James, the pastor of the church in Jerusalem, wrote this letter. He was well aware of the fact that if his people were to take a stand for Jesus, they would be persecuted from without and purified from within. He knew before long the Roman authorities would come in fury and anger, and soon they did. He confirmed with his people, however, that this also was God's plan for their lives. After all, was not their God stronger then the armies of Rome? You might ask, "Are you saying that God used Rome to build and deepen his people?" Absolutely! God has always used others to build and strengthen his church.

All through the history of Israel, God used those around them, not to destroy them, but to build them. God had the same plan for the early Christians as He does for our contemporaries. He did not allow so much persecution to come so as to dwarf or retard growth. He knew and knows today what to lay upon us, and how much we can endure in order to change us from weak saplings into mighty oak trees.

Jerry and his wife are not the worse for all of this. They are the better. I know they may not even know that now, but someday they will. James reminded his people in verse 3, *"Knowing this, that the trying of your faith worketh patience."* And in verse 4, *"But let patience have her perfect work, that ye may be perfect and entire, wanting nothing."* In other words, that they might be complete, needing nothing more to touch the hearts of others.

Isn't that a powerful thought, and have we not all seen it? Have you ever gone to a hospital to be a blessing, and come home having been blessed? Have you ever seen someone who ought not to be happy, yet were very happy indeed?

You see, when you are used of God to walk where so many others will walk, and you walk with an air of joy and peace, it will cause others to really take notice. That is what God is all about. He is building a kingdom. What your words and sermons don't seem to accomplish, your living example will! Saint Francis of Assisi once said, "Preach the Gospel all the time, everywhere, and to everyone, and when necessary, use words."

As the man James was martyred with the sword, though the Bible does not record it, I am sure he died in such a way that he led many more into the kingdom by his death than he ever could have by his life. Not only did God allow the persecution from without, He also allowed the suffering from within.

I remember, not long after I was saved, having read in I Peter 4:12-13, "*Beloved, think it not strange concerning the fiery trial which is to try you, as though some strange thing happened unto you: but rejoice, inasmuch as ye are partakers of Christ's sufferings; that, when his glory shall be revealed, he may be glad also with exceeding joy.*" In verse 19, "*Wherefore let them that suffer according to the will of God commit the keeping of their souls to him in well doing, as unto a faithful Creator.*"

There are several things that we notice immediately in this verse:

1. Don't be surprised when trouble comes.
2. Suffering is a master teacher.
3. Suffering has a master design.
4. Suffering has a major benefit.
5. Suffering can cause a major conflict.

Let's just mention one of these. Suffering can cause a major conflict in creating a bitter, not a better spirit. It is so easy, especially when the trial is very deep and extremely painful. The only way I know to keep from this, is to love Jesus enough to believe He does what is right and does not want to destroy us.

A Bitter Man

This past week I went to a little church in the state of Ohio. The church was located out in the rolling hills, far away from any metropolitan areas. When I arrived there on the first Sunday morning of our meetings, I found the church full of people both young and old. I felt impressed right at the start to be very careful and sensitive and to only try to encourage them to see Christ. It seemed that almost immediately there was a very receptive spirit. Not long into the week the pastor asked me if I would be willing to go and see a man for whom he was very burdened. I said I would be glad to go, but would like to know something about the situation. He told me this story:

It so happened that one year before we started these meetings, God really tested these believers. In this church there was a young man who was loved and respected by the other members, as well as by the entire community. He was a fine Christian and worked very hard at trying to get his friends and loved ones saved. The pastor said if there was a job to do in the church, this young man would most always volunteer, whether it be teaching a Sunday School Class, driving a bus or van or helping in house-to-house visitation. He could be counted on. It seemed that he had great and unusual athletic ability. Some felt that he would go on to college to play football and even have a chance at the professional ranks of the N.F.L. Just several weeks before his graduation from high school, he developed a pain in his jaw. It became so severe that his parents called the dentist and had him check his teeth. The dentist concluded that the young man needed to have four wisdom teeth extracted. He extracted them and sent him home to recover. The pain did not go away. It persisted until his

73

parents decided to take him to a general practitioner. The doctor checked him and found that he was running a high fever. He was sent to the hospital and from there flown to one of the best hospitals in the area. He was diagnosed as having an acute case of leukemia and died within a week. But he died with this testimony on his lips: "God knows what He is doing!"

One year later, his mother and sister were still suffering, but they were struggling to remain faithful. The father reacted in the opposite way. When his son—his only son—died, he couldn't handle it. Why *his* son? Why such a good boy? Why not the drug-heads and the dope dealers? Why would God come against his family? After all, they had given, within the past few years, their family, their business, and their future to God. Was this their reward? What else had he to give? The father stopped going to church and retreated into his thoughts and hurts and pretty much gave up on God.

After hearing this story, I sat there and asked God to give me wisdom before I spoke. I too have two sons. I wondered within myself, "Why?" I asked myself if I might not have reacted like this man. Then I thought about Jerry, the young man who had lost his son. He did not become bitter; he did not drop out of church, nor did he seem to accuse God of doing wrong. I wondered what made the difference. Perhaps the other man will come around. Perhaps this is just the time of transferring blame. Right now he has transferred it to God. Perhaps, just perhaps, he will come around.

I agreed to go by his business and talk to him, but only if he wanted to talk. We arrived at his office and before long he came in. I could tell right away that he was not in the mood to talk with us. The pastor introduced me and the man hesitantly extended his hand. We invited him to come to the meetings and left. I felt so bad for him. In fact, that night in my room, I was unable to sleep. I begged God to heal his hurting soul. He was a big man and maybe he had never allowed himself to weep and cleanse his emotions. As I lay there, I thought about his son and all the potential that was before him. It seemed as though God said to me, "Don't you think I need one of his kind to set as an example for others who are going through the same ordeal?" Yes, God was looking for a pattern to lay down, so that others could walk and find their way to Him.

In Acts 14:22 we read, *"That we must through much tribulation enter into the kingdom of God."*

Perhaps this verse is no consolation when we look at and anticipate the future. But it is fact, and it is reality. That is what I appreciate about God's Word. It does not try to cover up or disguise reality. Satan does that. He glamorizes sin; he dresses up death, and he makes error appear as truth. Philosophy does the same, but when faced with reality, it cannot stand. Our religion can, and will stand. Our hope carries us beyond our hurt and through our despair. Thank God, weeping may endure for the night, but joy cometh in the morning! Isn't this the message the world needs? How can we who know the truth keep silent? We must tell the old, old story, and the story is not that we do not hurt, or that we *will not* hurt, but that *one day* we shall not hurt. "Some glorious daybreak, Jesus will come. Some glorious daybreak, battles all done. We'll fight the victory, break through the blue, some glorious morning for me, for you."

Don't you often wonder what people do who do not know Jesus? Who cares for their troubled hearts? To whom do they go? I guess we know what they do. They turn to drugs, excessive behavior, and violence. These are all the alternatives for men, women, boys, and girls who have turned from Jesus, who is the only real source of hope and help.

In closing this chapter, we must take to heart the admonition of Pastor James. We must not only carry our Bibles and read them, but we must learn how to implement or put the Bible into our lives. We must live it! We will then become Missouri Christians. Oh, how many people are looking for direction and help. We must not fail them!

Why don't you pause right now and ask God to help you in a better and deeper way to live what you know. Why don't you ask God to give you some verses that apply to your situation, and then apply them and practice them? Try Isaiah 26:3-4, *"Thou wilt keep him in perfect peace, whose mind is stayed on thee, because he trusteth in thee, Trust ye in the Lord forever; for in the Lord God is everlasting strength."*

May God be your strength!

Chapter 5
Seeing God in Your Service

As we come to this chapter, allow me to once again remind you of the basic purpose of this writing. Remember how we stated that we all from time to time come to situations and events in life that leave us with no other response than to ask why? I had heard early in my Christian walk that it was a sin to ask why. I really could identify with this philosophy having been in the Marine Corps. There is a saying in the Marine Corp which goes like this: "Yours is not to reason why, yours is just to do or die." So when good-meaning people said the same thing to me concerning the Christian life I just said, "Yes sir!"

But I have come to discover that condemning someone for asking why is just not right. In fact, I now realize the opposite to be true.

We have already stated that God is working His wonders to perform in strange and at times even perplexing ways. However, as we sit down and consider the testimonies that are in the Bible, it helps us to see, to understand, and be satisfied.

We conclude along with the Apostle James that when we come into these dark valleys of despair and confusion, God wants us to freely come to Him to gain wisdom. We are to come and ask our father, "Why?" The

Christian life is not like the Marine Corps in which we are to be fearful followers only to do what we are told and die if we don't. Our Savior is not a drill instructor barking out commands that we arbitrarily obey and must not ever have the audacity to question.

Beloved, our Lord wants us to be wise in our dealings with Him and He wants us to know why He is leading us in such or such a way.

We have previously seen that in order to help us with this wisdom, we need to see Him in His sovereignty. Sometimes, He truly works in ways that are entirely foreign to us. He has the privilege of seeing the whole picture and has an ultimate plan that most often transcends our present life and sojourn here on earth.

In His sovereignty we can begin to understand this thing called suffering. Though we may never fully understand it all now, as we trust His heart we can accept what comes from His hands, and the way He works out His plan.

Service

Now as we come to this chapter on service we must be just as keen and sensitive to God as we are when we are suffering or trying to understand the sovereignty of the one we serve.

We are all called to serve. In fact, the last commandment Jesus gave to us was one of service. Some call this the Great Commission; I am not sure it is a commissioning service as much as it is a commanding service. Certainly from this point the disciples did not go into immediate service. Just because someone gives orders does not mean that everyone enlists in the Army. There is a time when one presents oneself for service, and at that time we can call it a commissioning service. We who are Christians are under the mandate of God to serve Him. As soon as one says, "Yes, Lord, I will serve you in my life," Satan becomes very unhappy. He then will do whatever he can to hinder and, if he can, to destroy one's ambition.

So when we talk about service what we mean is serving God, whether it be as a Sunday School teacher, a leader in the church, a witness for Christ, or encouraging the work and workers of God. Whatever the capacity, we all are under mandate from God to serve.

We must once again be reminded that even in our service, the one thing that God is doing in our lives is making a blueprint, an example, a pathway for those who will follow to have as their guide and encouragement. Paul said in II Corinthians 2:2, *"Ye are our epistles written in our hearts, known and read of all men."* Paul calls these Corinthians living letters for people to read. You know, I wish I would have truly understood that when I first went into full-time service. Somehow, I think it would have been so much easier for me. However, I soon noticed how comforting and reassuring it was for me as I heard others tell of experiences which were familiar to me and how God's grace was sufficient for them. Their encouragement to me was, "Reverend Arnold, if God was able to help me, He will be sufficient in your need also." I realize now that God was in it all and sufficient to supply all my needs as I entered this incredible war zone.

Chapter 6
The War Zone

"Finally my brethren be strong in the Lord and in the power of His might. Put on the whole armor of God that ye might be able to stand against the wiles of the devil."

Ephesians 6:10-11

Victor Hugo's story "93" tells of 93 crew members that are being tossed about in a very violent storm which threatens their lives. The captain is doing everything he can to save the ship by instructing the crew to throw everything overboard that is not necessary for their survival. At some point in the midst of this storm, the captain became sore concerned by something he was hearing down in the ships hold. He sent two of the crew to investigate. What they found was that one of the large canons had broken from its moorings and was being tossed violently from side to side, threatening to break a hole in the ship. The captain commanded two men to go below and do whatever necessary to secure the cannon. He told them that if they didn't secure the cannon, they would be destroyed from within rather than from without. "We are like that ship. Our souls are more imperiled by the inward power of sin than by the outer storms of the world and the devil."[7]

Not long after I had accepted my first church assignment, I came face to face with the reality of actual ministry. Somehow, in my thinking I had not really come to grips with what the ministry was all about. Oh, yes, I had read about the Apostle Paul's ministry and how he had suffered and was beaten and even killed, it was thought. But somehow it never dawned on me that I would have to contend with these or similar challenges. I too would need to put on the whole armor of God each day, that I too might be able to stand against the enemy. Somehow I just didn't grasp that. I guess I figured that these were different times and those things just didn't happen anymore. What a shock! What a lie of the devil!

Once, early in my ministry, a man who was a bitter Christian came to see me. He had deep feelings of resentment against many people, including myself. You see, he had given the land upon which we hoped to build a church. He had actually been the one who was instrumental in organizing the church and having a constitution drawn up and finally papers of Incorporation, giving our church the proper legal foundation. Though he always said he did not want to be the pastor, deep down in his heart he really hoped the people would vote him in. He didn't have much of a formal education, but he was, I believe, a good man and had a sincere desire to serve God. After all, he had done more than all the other thirty-some members in trying to get the little flock organized and the ministry off the ground.

---

[7] Boa, Kenneth; Conformed to His Image. Zondervan Publishing. Grand Rapids, MI, 2001, p.330. Victor Hugo's story

Because people were oblivious to his true desire, they called a young man right out of Bible school. Due to the pressure placed on him by this bitter man, the young man resigned within a matter of months. Then it was my turn. I, too, had just graduated from college and was very naïve. I was perhaps less prepared concerning the overall ministry and, in particular, this kind of a situation. I walked head-long into a place I think angels would have feared to tread.

I was not there long before this man stirred up the flocks, and within seven months I was asked to resign. As I reflect on it now, this causes me to chuckle in my heart. At the time though, it almost destroyed me. One evening, shortly after our evening meal, I received a phone call from the chairman of the Board of Deacons. Now, when you receive a call from this man, you know there is serious business at hand. But, being the novice that I was, I thought that, perhaps, because I had been preaching such dynamic sermons and was teaching so many deep truths, that he probably wanted to come to my house with a raise or at least some congratulations. So, when he asked if he could come, I was ecstatic with anticipation.

Brother, my bubble was soon broken when this man announced to my wife and I that he and the other four deacons had prayed and felt God told them I was to leave. Can you imagine how that hit me? I was a green-horn and basically trusted every Christian and believed that the church was filled with God-fearing and God-loving people. I really did. I thought if there was any one place on earth that was close to perfection, it was most certainly the church. Surely these people could and would look over failures and shortcomings. Surely, if anyone would go the extra mile, it would be church people. Now, here was supposedly the most spiritual man of the congregation handing me my resignation. I had only been there a little over seven months.

I was stunned, hurt, and I guess embarrassed by it all. And my wife sat there, having to hear that her husband was already a failure in his profession. What could I say? Should I ask for a second chance? Should I plead ignorance, or what? What should I do? Where was I to go? Should I get angry? In the world, that is what I would always do. When I failed, I would get angry and would try to transfer blame. This, however, was the ministry and I was expected to react Christ-like. I felt desperation grip me. I had a handicapped son and a small daughter. I sat there, mystified. What should I say? Now, honestly, here is what I asked this man.

"Sir, did God tell you and the others where I am to go?"

I could tell immediately that he was taken back. He began to stutter and stumble and said,

"We don't really know that."

He then said, "You will have to decide that."

"No," I said, "You are the ones God has spoken to about this. You go back to God, and when you find out where I am to go, let me know. As soon as I know where God wants me to go, I will be glad to get away from the likes of you."

The man jumped up and said, "You have heard our decision," and left with the door rattling.

Why was this happening to me? I know I was probably a pitiful preacher and even less of an administrator, but I wanted to do the will of God.

The deacon had made several accusations that hurt me. The one that hurt the most was, "You are a leader, leading the blind." Was I, really? Was what he was saying about me true? Certainly, when people accuse you like this, you should ask and search yourself to see if it is true. After all, we all have blind spots and shortcomings that oftentimes others can see better than we can.

I sat there that evening and far into the early morning peering into the darkness, hoping that somewhere in the gloom God would show Himself and come to me with assurance and direction. My dear wife tried to assure me that I was not a blind leader. Then, God bless her, she began to break under pressure. She could not stand to see her husband humiliated and almost destroyed emotionally. She tried to stay strong, but I could see her weaken little by little. I began to falter and to entertain the idea of getting out of the ministry. I wanted to run and hide.

I was in the war zone.

Our Foundation

Archimedes, the Greek mathematician (287-212 BC) said, "Give me a place to stand and I can move the world."[8] I interpret this to mean that by means of a lever and a proper fulcrum and a foundation upon which to plant his feet, a man could accomplish wonders. Certainly Christians are no different. We need to have our feet planted on a firm foundation so as to stand against all that will come against us. The foundation for

---

[8] S.E. Anderson, Our Inerrant Bible. Bogard Press, Texarkana, Texas p.39-40 1977

the Christian is the Holy Scriptures. Dr. W.A. Criswell, the pastor of First Baptist Church of Dallas, Texas, said concerning the word of God:

> "The word of God is like God Himself, eternal and unchanging. There is a transiency, illusion and decay in all that is human and mundane. There is an ultimate and certain ruin awaiting all human works, the efforts and building of all human hands. But reason requires, and our souls cry out for some all unalterable, unchanging stratum below all the fleeting phenomena of this changing world. We are driven back, back, back, by the very fact of the temporal and transient, to grasp for a refuge in the immutable and the permanent. Where can we find it–the foundation rock that cannot be moved? We find that rock in God and in His word".[9]

The scholarly and devout B.B. Warfield once said, "The Bible is the word of God in such a way that when the Bible speaks, God speaks."[10]

"In times like these, we need a Savior, in times like these we need an anchor. Be very sure, be very sure, your anchor holds and grips that solid rock. This rock is Jesus, yes, he's the one. This rock is Jesus, the only one. Be very sure, be very sure, your anchor holds and grips that solid rock."

---

[9] Criswell, W.A. These Issues We Must Face p. 87 quoted in S.E. Anderson. Our inerrant Bible Bogard Press, Texarkana, Texas 1977 p 75

[10] Zuck Roy, B. Basic Bible Interpretation: A practical Guide to Discovering Biblical Truth. David C. Cook Publishing, Colorado Springs, CO,1991. p 9.

So often songs like this one are mere verses and tunes, but not quite reality. So often, we just sing hymns and never think about what we are saying. This song seemed to come to me in the midst of my war zone. I began to think about these words and what they meant. Were they really true or were they just a nice song to sing in church?

I was certainly convinced that I needed much more than I possessed. I knew I needed Jesus if I were to keep from drowning in my own sea of self-pity. It hurt!

Was Jesus a foundation, a rock, *a rock to which I could cling?* I heard many say he was, now it was my turn to find out. If He was, did I have my anchor firmly gripping Him?

I realized I had to once again affirm my faith in his sovereignty and had to be reassured that his grace was sufficient enough to heal my hurt.

I went alone to my office. I closed the door and entered into a precious time with Jesus. I told him my hurts, and how I had been treated, and how I was ready to quit and do something else, and how I was really trying to do my best. When I finished presenting my case, it was as though a still small voice within me said: *You didn't need to tell me, I know it.* Wow! He knew all about it. He had heard the conversations, the accusations, and the thoughts of quitting. Wow! The eyes of the Lord had been running to and fro, beholding it all. I wept, and said, "I am sorry." He then seemed to say, "Just hold onto me, stand on me, lean on me, I will be your strength." That time with God was so special to me that I emerged from my office never again to doubt that my Lord was watching over my path and noticing it all.

In your service for God you, too, must never doubt that God is aware of it all. He is an ever-ready help, especially in a time of trouble. You too, must once again make sure that you are standing firmly on God's foundation. That foundation is His Word. In Psalms 11:3, David asked this question, "If the foundation be destroyed what can the righteous do?" In other words, the only hope for any of us is the hope we have in God's Holy Word. It must always be the final authority. We cannot make it on our own. Sooner or later, the wisdom of man will come up short and leave us woefully inadequate. You see, it was God's word that caused the first-century Christians, as well as all the others from Pentecost until now, to be victorious. They simply believed what God said. They had experienced and witnessed the power of the resurrected Christ and went forth under His authority.

Perhaps one of the best examples I can think of regarding the importance of God's Word in a man's life is the story we find in the Book of Ecclesiastes of a dilemma in King Solomon's life. This man, as you perhaps remember, had a special meeting with God. The meeting took place at a time when the king was in a very difficult period of his life. He was trying to be a good king for God's people, but the work was becoming too much for him. God came to him and said, "Ask me for one thing and I will do it for you." King Solomon said, "Lord, give me wisdom, that I might know how to lead the people." God granted it to him and he has since been referred to as the wisest man who ever lived.

However, after many years of faithful service and having been in the war zone for so long, he began to forget wherein His strength lay. He began to think like many of his contemporaries. Due to specific areas of life that he allowed to go unchecked, this king began to live and reign in the energy of his own strength and feelings.

We will all battle with these temptations when the heat is really on us. It is imperative in these circumstances that we have real discipline in our lives and we must somehow see God behind it all. Donald Whitney makes this comment in his book *Spiritual Disciplines*, "Discipline without direction is drudgery."[11] In other words, in order for discipline to have its perfect work, there must be a goal or an objective that we hope to achieve. That goal, I believe, should be that in all things we might be conformed more and more to the image of Christ (Romans 8:29). Whitney perhaps describes it even better when he says, "Whatever the discipline, its most important feature is its purpose. Just as there is little value in practicing scales on a guitar or piano apart from the purpose of playing music, there is little value in practicing spiritual disciplines apart from the single purpose that unites them and that purpose is godliness. Thus we are told in I Timothy 4:7, *"But refuse profane and old wives-fables, and exercise (discipline) thyself rather unto godliness."*[12]

Another way to say it is that it really is not about us, IT IS ALL ABOUT GOD. In chapter 12 of Ecclesiastes, the king finally came to grips with the foundation of God's Word and God's leading. What a lesson for us all. Make sure that in the midst of your war zone you don't lose confidence

---

[11] Whitney, Donald, S. Spiritual Disciplines for the Christian Life. Nav Press; Colorado Springs, Colorado, 1994, p. 5

[12] Ibid, p.7

in God and the fact that God is using you in a very unique way to be that pattern that others after you might be able to follow.

In Ecclesiastes 12:5, it seems as though King Solomon finally comes to his senses. He then deals with three fundamental questions that have been asked by man from the foundation of the world: (1) Where did I come from? (2) Why am I here? (3) Where am I going? The first question, "Where did I come from?", is answered in verse 7. We have come from God, we have not evolved. We are not merely the result of the gene pools from our parents. But we have been made and designed by God. Psalm 139:16 says, *"Thine eyes did see my substance yet being unperfected; and in thy book all my members were written, which in continuance were fashioned when as yet there were none of them"*. Even in your mother's womb, God was at work making you, forming you. You must believe that you are unique and that you have been created to fulfill many divine purposes many of which we will not fully understand until we cross to the other side.

The second question is, "Why am I here?" In Ecclesiastes 12:13 King Solomon said, *"Let us hear the conclusion of the whole matter: fear God and keep his commandments, for this is the whole duty of man."* We can conclude that we are to fear our God. That does not mean we cringe in fear of Him, but rather that we stand in awe even thinking of Him. He is so sovereign that even in making and forming this majestic earth in which we find ourselves He merely spoke, and the beauty and perfection came immediately into being. This is the same God that is overlooking you and me and is in total control of all the affairs of men. In part B of this same statement, we are to keep his laws until the very breath is taken from us.

You see, it is not about you or me. This world must really be about God and His incredible plan for us. It is so easy to say "It is not about me," but the reality is that it is happening to *me* and the difficulties and the trials are pressing on *me*. They are the burdens that I must bear. It is in this war zone that I must believe that God is intimately at work, helping me to conform, that I might be a pattern for Jesus.

My son David was born with cerebral palsy. We did not realize that until two years after his birth. We knew he was different, and since he was born prematurely we just assumed that he was slower in development. My wife and I had been struggling with God's specific will for our lives. I was studying at Bob Jones University to become a teacher. However, the longer I sat under the influence of godly men who came to the university to speak, I felt God was calling me to a different area of ministry. I certainly never believed that God would want me to be a preacher. I did not feel that I had the gifts or sensed a particular calling or a desire for that area of work. In the local church where Gloria and I were attending, an evangelist came to speak in the latter part of October. One evening, he talked about surrendering to the will of God. His theme was "dying to self." He used the passage from Philippians where Paul said "I die daily." We were encouraged to ask God to help us to die to our own passions and desires and ask to have His desire.

It is not easy to die to self. In fact it is impossible, categorically, to die to that part of our human nature. God does not want us to become robots and have a passive outlook in our daily living. I sensed that God was asking me to be willing to be what He wanted me to be, go where He wanted me to go, and do whatever it was that He would desire. It seemed as though I had the peace of God to take that step of surrender. My wife and I went forward and we knelt at the altar, asking God to give us grace. We both went home that evening with an enormous amount of peace in our hearts.

Several weeks later, seemingly out of nowhere, our son David was crawling across the floor and he began to cry. Not a normal cry, but a cry of pain. When I went to pick him up I touched his arm and I realized that he had somehow hurt it. We went to the hospital and after a doctor's diagnosis, they discovered that Davie had cracked a bone in his arm. He was put in a cast and we returned one month later to have his arm examined. It was healed, but the doctor asked us to come to his office for a consultation. While there, he asked me, "David, I guess you realize that your son will never be a Mickey Mantle." I was flabbergasted, I wondered what he meant. He then asked, "Do you realize your son has cerebral palsy?"

My friend, I could never in my human ability express to you my hurt. Why would God allow this in our lives after we surrendered to His will? Was there something else to which we had to die? Was this our reward for surrendering to our Lord?

After several days of struggling with this new information, we felt assured in our hearts through II Corinthians 1, that God was going to comfort us in our hurt so that we would be able to comfort others who were suffering in the same way. Were we willing to enter into this arena of suffering so that we could be a pattern and example for many others that were living around us?

Years later, God called us to a little village, Kreamer, PA, to pastor a house church. Several miles down the road from the church was a large institution that I came to discover was a hospital for cerebral palsy patients. There were over 700 people in that hospital. God enabled us to work with these patients, which in turn provided opportunities to minister to many people around the state which included, in one instance, a U.S. Senator and his wife. Truly God worked in mysterious ways, His wonders to perform.

Thirdly, "Where are we going?" King Solomon states in verse 7, *"Then shall the dust return to the earth as it was: and the spirit shall return unto God WHO GAVE IT,"* (emphasis mine). This realm is referred to in the scriptures as *eternity*, meaning that it has no beginning it has no end and it is not limited by time or space. In eternity, there are two distinct realms. One is the eternal kingdom of heaven where all the saved on earth will go. The other is the kingdom of hell and judgment where souls go who have rejected Christ, or perhaps thought they could delay acceptance another day. In order for people to enter into the kingdom of God, they must be born again by the spirit of God.

John 3:16 makes it very clear that men do not go to heaven because of good works or miss heaven because of bad works, but rather by receiving or rejecting the gift of God. In John 3, a religious man came to Jesus and said, *"'Rabbi, we know that thou art a teacher come from God, for no man can do these miracles that thou doest except God be with him.' Jesus answered and said, 'Verily I say unto thee except a man be born again he cannot see the kingdom of God.'"* Though Nicodemus was a religious man, he needed to accept Christ as his Savior and Lord and ask for forgiveness of his sins to receive eternal life.

The other realm is the realm of the unforgiven and the damned for all eternity. In John 5:28-29 we read, *"Marvel not at this: for the hour is coming, in the which all that are in the graves shall hear his voice, and shall come forth; they that have done good unto the resurrection of life; and they that have done evil, unto the resurrection of damnation."* The good works that are mentioned here are not the good works in the sense of doing good deeds. But rather, having done that which God has previously said we must do. That is, merely confessing that we are sinners and asking God to save us. Oh, how simple that is and yet how man and religion has so greatly complicated it. Perhaps if there is any one area with which we battle most, it is this earth and clay which houses our spirit. When you really think about it, all suffering, disease, and hardships are common to this earth and vessel. The most sacred and eternal part of you, your spirit, can and must remain the same. It is your spirit that will one day rise from the earthen vessel and return to the eternal kingdom and receive eternal glory and praise. *"That the suffering of this present time is not worthy to be compared with the glory which shall be revealed in us,"* (Romans 8:18).

Everywhere I have traveled, I have seen and heard men asking these questions and searching for answers. In India, they search for them hoping to find answers in sacrifice, self-denial and self-inflicted suffering. One Hindu man I saw refused to lie down for one year hoping to appease the gods (of which there are thousands) for his suffering on Judgment Day. Babies are still being sacrificed to appease and find grace. The first-born son is often neglected so that he becomes sickly and eventually is put into the Ganges River to find grace.

Master Builder/Chief Designer

In verse 11, Solomon makes reference to the One who is ultimately in control and orchestrating this universe and unfolding human drama. The chief designer is called the Master of Assembly. Now we all can understand this description. We have all seen an assembly line, either in a picture or from personal experience. We have seen how the set-up and all the workers are on a course designed to build a product. As the line continues to move along, it goes through various departments where new things are added until it becomes a completed product. Most importantly, however, is that there is a master designer behind it all. His work was done first. This is neither the result of random changes nor an evolution of chance. This all speaks of a designer. King Solomon now clarifies the matter concerning life and definitively authenticates a designer behind the universe and, in particular, our lives. He is saying God is at work in the good times and in the bad times. Ephesians 2:10 says, *"For we are his workmanship, created in Christ Jesus unto good works, which God had ordained that we should walk in them."*

Solomon then becomes more specific in telling us how God goes about such a major undertaking. You will notice he uses two objects to best describe his methods. He uses the words "goads" and "nails" fastened by the Master Builder.

Goads were long slender sticks with sharp instruments fastened to the end. They were used to control the oxen or the asses when working in the fields or pulling loads of cargo from one place to another. The workers would be able to get the animals to go in the direction he wanted simply by applying pressure to one side of the animal or the other.

Nails were also very familiar because of the importance in securing tents from the fierce winds that would arise in the desert. They spoke of security and foundation.

King Solomon wants to show how God works His careful design in us, His people, as well as the methods He employs, and therefore uses these familiar terms. Beloved, it is the same today. As God's people, we must make sure that we are standing secure on the foundation of God's Word. It is only here that we will be able to resist the strong winds of adversity as well as the incredible winds of change. All of these will come against us and try to destroy us or at least move us from the only foundation that can cause us to stand.

Secondly, we must understand that even when we are in the perfect will of God, or should I say, the place we feel God would have us to be, the Master Designer will sometimes use sharp testings and trials, such as these goads, to get us to move on or to go in another direction. And this, my friend, if you are not careful, can be a very discouraging time and even cause ultimate defeat in your life. It is during this time you should seek wisdom from a multitude of counselors. But, ultimately, the final counsel must come from your personal time with God.

A perfect illustration of this is in I Kings 17. Elijah had been warned by God that there was going to be a three-year drought. God told him to go hide himself by the brook Cherith and to drink its water and then concluded by saying that He had commanded the ravens to feed him. And this they did. They brought bread and flesh in the morning and bread and flesh in the evening. The Bible then says in verse 7, *"After a while the brook dried up."* Now, this was not the result of God's judgment, nor because He was just unconcerned. No, God had another plan for Elijah's life. There was a woman who needed his help, a widow in Zarephath who needed his ministry. God was now expanding his ministry, not destroying it.

In our service, we must ever keep in mind that where we are today may not be where we will be tomorrow. God works in strange ways.

Last evening here in Western, Ohio, just before I got up to preach, the pastor gave an illustration that set the tone for a meeting with God. He introduced a woman in the audience and told about her life and, in particular, about one of her sons. When he was just 10 years of age, he was introduced to drugs by his older brother. This young lad got so bad they could not do anything with him. He would steal and rob peoples' houses and had even attempted murder. Things got to a point that he was facing juvenile detention. In a time of plea bargaining, this mother asked for permission for her son to go to a Christian home in Texas for help. The mother had just become a Christian herself had been told of this place called The Lester Roloff Home for Boys. The judge, frustrated with the juvenile, agreed to give him another chance.

The results were phenomenal. Before long, this young man wrote home and told how he had become a Christian and how he was studying his Bible and even memorizing large portions of it. He stayed there for several years and then returned home. When he got there, he told his mother he felt God wanted him to become a preacher and work with young men like himself.

He made several inquiries into Christian colleges, but was not accepted because of his poor grades and lack of a high school diploma. The pastor told how he then became discouraged and went back to drinking. On one of these occasions, he came to the pastor and told him he was thinking about taking his life and wanted to know if he would still go to heaven. The pastor told him God hated suicide, but that if he was truly saved he would go to heaven. Several days later, he took his life. At the funeral, the church was filled with narcotic people as well as many friends.

On the front row, sitting beside his mother was his older brother who had introduced him to drugs, and had just been paroled from prison. When the invitation was given to accept Christ and make sure of his soul's salvation, this brother was the first to raise his hand along with some 80% of the other people in attendance. The pastor concluded by saying that perhaps in his death, this young man did more than in his life. This older brother later surrendered his life to take up his brother's mantel and is now in Bible college, training for the ministry.

Now, as to just how God worked in this, only He really knows. How much of it was His doing, only He knows. One thing that is sure is that God is still the Master Designer, and we must be convinced and content to let him bring His design to pass.

Our service will be effective only as we see Him in it all. Not only is it important to realize the importance of our foundation, but we must also be assured that our God never calls a man to do something without giving him the wherewithal to do it.

Mysterious Plans

Oft times when we are going through experiences we might think "surely none of this could be of God," or "God would never work like this." Certainly He would not allow children to be born and raised in a difficult environment where there would be potential for them to become something far from what God would desire. For instance, when I think back on my home life I have often wondered why God would have allowed me to live in difficult circumstances—such as an alcoholic home—when now, years later, I believe I see the picture much better. God did not design this plan, but He permitted this plan in my life that I would have compassion and understand people coming from the same environment.

My home setting and background cause me most often to have deep feelings of inferiority and poor self-esteem. I was born and raised in a home where my father drank a lot and was very abusive to my mother. His drinking problem produced many hardships on our family and caused us to have many needs. When I was nine years old, my father, a young man of 47, died and left my mother with very little on which to raise her three children. She had to struggle and work hard just to keep body and soul together. We never had much of a home life, because of my dear mother's long work hours. We did not study or pay much attention to our school work. We all got through, but certainly not with very much respect. In fact, one teacher told me I would be a drunk like my father. I can still remember the hurt, but thought her statement was probably the truth. However, my mother pleaded with me for as long as I can remember to promise her I would not drink and bring that shame to her again. I loved her and never wanted to cause her any more hardship and pain. I watched her as she took in other peoples' washing and ironing to care for us. I saw her climb snow drifts to hang up clothing at night, and often before she would get them hung they would begin to get stiff like boards and freeze. I promised her and God I would never break her heart.

I remember just after my father died that my grandmother came to visit us. She was a very wicked woman and so different than my mother, that I had a hard time believing she was actually my mother's mother. I know it is not nice to say things like this about your family, but truth is truth. During that particular visit, in front of my sister and I, she said to my mother, "Alice, why don't you put these kids in a home so you don't have to work so hard." Oh, how that hurt us. We went to our rooms and cried. We feared that our mother might become so weary with her life that she would give in to my grandmother's suggestion.

As soon as our grandmother left, we went down to talk to our mother. She assured us she would never do something like that, but that we would need to help her where we could and not cause her any more burdens. We promised, and I can say today that though I was certainly not perfect, I really never ever talked back to my mother and always tried to do what she asked.

This background did, however, leave me with a feeling of being a cut beneath. I always felt inferior. The year my father died, I was in third grade. He died in April and in May I failed my year. The teacher, for whatever reason, did not like me. She would have me stand before the class and say, "David, your brain is no bigger than this," and she would hold her two fingers apart just so you could see through. Time and time again she would say that to me before the entire class. I started to believe her and, consequently, did very poorly in the next year and then into the fourth year which she also taught.

When I entered fifth grade, my life changed dramatically. I had a teacher who showed me love and gave me special attention. During the winter she would ask me to help her home at night. Often she would invite me into her home for some of her sugar cookies and milk. She never told me about Christ, but gave me an appreciation for classical music and during the Christmas season had me listen to the Messiah. I believe in her own way she was witnessing to me. She was an incredible instrument God was using to mold my life and perhaps ultimately bring me to Himself.

When I graduated from high school, no one ever expected me to be successful at anything. God certainly had other plans. It was while I was in the United States Marine Corps that I, through my wife Gloria (who was just a friend then), found Christ. From the Marine Corps I enrolled in Bob Jones University with the intention of being a coach and health teacher. However, after struggling, I felt a tugging toward the ministry in my heart for some time. To say the least, when many of my friends heard that I was studying for the ministry, they almost died of shock.

So, coming into the ministry I had a lot of baggage I needed to let go of somehow. In particular, the feelings of being inferior and not being too smart. I struggled much with these, but thank God, before I went into the real war zone in my first pastorate, God gave me some truths. I have used them as goads to point me in the right direction and the basis of a foundation on which to build.

God Enables

"A man's gift maketh room for him, and bringeth him before great men." Proverbs 18:16

I shall never forget the impact this verse had on me after I asked God to help me, because I felt so inadequate in my ministry. He seemed to show me that He had given me gifts and that it was *my* responsibility to hone them. He promised me that He had done his part and I was to do mine. So I set out to study and polish the gifts he had given to me. To my absolute surprise, I started to see God work through me and on several occasions I knew God had just worked a miracle.

People started to come to my little church. It grew from a tiny beginning to a church known all over the state of Pennsylvania. People were saved, families restored, sick people were made well, and many things occurred that had no human explanation.

God had given me gifts and it was up to me to do my part. For you who read this book, God has given you gifts too. Don't worry about how God could use you, just do the preparation that is yours to do, hone your gift and leave the rest up to God. I did not set out to have a great church, a big church, or a big name. I only wanted to do my best and not be a failure. And somehow I wanted to feel good about myself. God did that and so much more. You see, He said, "I will take the simple [plain things] of this world to confound the wise, that the glory should go to God and not man."

God was at work all the time, even in my early home life. God allowed me to see my father as he would literally crawl home on his hands and knees when drunk. This caused me to hate alcohol with a passion and to warn all of its evils. He allowed me to have a humble beginning so that I would know the hurt of a humble home. How else could I go to others, understand them and empathize with them if I had not been through what they had? And most of all, God allowed me the privilege to watch a young widow of 36 deny her own pleasures and ambitions and live for her kids. I saw her go to bed late and rise early. I saw her with only a few clothes in her closet and yet she never, never complained. I watched her give her food to her children and say, "I am not hungry today," when now I am sure she was more concerned with our health than her own. Yes, God let all these goads come into my life not to dwarf me or hurt me, but to accomplish His workmanship. Again, the purpose was to deepen me and broaden me, and to use me as a pattern for those coming from the same background as mine.

Today, I realize God was giving me a gift of exhortation and encouragement. I had been so sensitive to anyone who would reach out to me, that I guess I wanted to be one who would reach to the out-of-the-way people, and ask, "May I help you?" Beloved, do you see it? God is making a body. In that body there are many parts, all of which are important.

According to Scripture, there are 12 different gifts. These are recorded in Romans 12:3-16 and I Corinthians 12:4-11. These gifts are given by God. Gifts and talents are not the same. Gifts are tools God gives. Talents are natural bends that people have. Talents can be worked with and improved. Gifts are given by an act of God. When trying to define the difference, it is sometimes difficult, but when you see or hear them there is no mistake. Perhaps it can be best explained by the example of a talented Shakespearian performer.

A man was invited to a town to recite Shakespearian prose. As he spoke, he held the audience speechless. When he finished, people stood to their feet and broke into applause. There was an old preacher who was known to them all. He was asked if he would come to the stage and quote the 23rd Psalm and close in prayer. When he finished quoting the Psalm, the people stood with tears in their eyes and said, "What a Savior!" There is a difference. Don't ever try to fake a gift, but seek God to find out the gifts God has given to you. When you discover your gift, do the best that you can to hold onto it and make it a ready instrument that God can use.

God Performs

Now this second part of Proverbs 18:16 says, *"A man's gift maketh room for him, and bringeth him before great men."* When God led me to this passage in Proverbs, He said, "David, I will equip you, and in my timing I will elevate you and even bring you before great men. You do your part and I will do mine."

Brothers and sisters, I have preached to literally thousands of people at one time. I have had in my audience ex-governors, and I have governors and judges as personal friends. I have stood before 7,000 young people at Northern Arizona State University in Flagstaff, Arizona, and watched God work in a wonderful way. I have met heads of state and have traveled around the world several times and preached on every continent–not bad for that poor boy who was raised on the banks of the Juniata River in Millerstown, PA. Yes, God is so good and He not only loves me, but He loves you as well. All we must do is die to ourselves, our ambitions, our ideas of success, our sin, allow him to live through us, and be patient.

I have now been in the service of God for over 45 years and am convinced that all of the avenues he has led me in and through were for the betterment of my service. My life has made me solid in my convictions, humble in my walk, and sensitive and sympathetic in my dealings with others.

Yes, the Christian life is truly a war zone. The battle rages every second, or at least it seems that way sometimes. Temptations are so subtle, urging us to quit, to be fearful, to be sinful, to be unfaithful. *"For He hath made Him to be sin for us, who knew no sin; that we might be made the righteousness of God in Him,"* (II Corinthians 5:21). But thanks be to God who causeth us to be more than conquerors through him who loved us.

You too must be faithful in your service for God. He did not make you to serve the world, the flesh, and the devil. He made you for His glory. You are His creation. Doesn't He deserve your service? If you have failed in the past, God will forgive you. All you need to do is to come back to him and be honest. Don't lie when you pray and say, "God, I love you." Say, "God, I don't love you. I haven't been concerned with your business. Please forgive me."

If you are not sure you are saved, come to him today. Come just as you are, a sinner, and ask for forgiveness. John 6:37 says, *"All that the Father giveth me shall come to me; and him that cometh to me I will in no wise cast out."* He does not love some and hate others. He loves all and wants everyone to be saved. II Peter 3:9, *"The Lord is not slack concerning his promise, as some men count slackness; but is longsuffering to us-ward, not willing that any should perish, but that all should come to repentance."*

Yes, for service or salvation, Jesus is waiting. Won't you come to him just now?

Chapter 7
Weary Christian syndrome

"But they that wait upon the Lord shall renew their strength;

they shall mount up with wings as eagles; they shall run,

and not be weary; and they shall walk, and not faint."

Isaiah 40:31

Dr. Bob Jones Senior used to tell us preacher boys that it was not a sin to be down in the dumps, but it was a sin to stay there. He also said, "You cannot keep the buzzards from flying over your head, but you can keep them from roosting in your hair," and that "Weariness is common to man, but how important it is that we deal with a weary state of being."

In this chapter, the prophet Isaiah is reminding the people of Israel who had become weary in their well-doing that they could indeed be renewed to strength and victory if they would learn to wait upon the Lord. When you become aware of a preacher, a Sunday School teacher, or a Christian worker stating that they need to resign because of all the pressure and burden of the work, they are merely stating the fact—even though they may not know it—that they are not having the proper fellowship with their Lord. It is in this critical time and vulnerable state that Satan will attack in a very subtle way to cause you to cast doubt upon the integrity of God.

You see, my friends, you cannot sufficiently wait on someone if you are suspicious of him.

Just like back in the garden of Eden, Satan was able to remove Eve from her position of trust by causing her to doubt that God really was fair and just. You cannot wait, in an hour of great testing, if you doubt whether He really does care or if He can make a difference in our lives. The children of Israel had lost confidence in their God and many of them had become idolaters and, eventually, adulterers.

The tragedy of this setting was that the promise of waiting upon God and being renewed by Him was not possible for these people unless they came back to the initial state of being confident in His ability to work miracles. Waiting demands love, trust, and confidence. So rather than throwing in the towel and giving up in our ministries, we must learn to wait for God to come again with refreshing latter rains to refresh our wearily burdened heart. What does it mean to wait upon the Lord? Does it mean that we drop out of the race, we go away and sit under the proverbial gourd as Jonah did, sulking and drowning in his self pity? No! No! Not at all!

The word *wait* has four connotative meanings in the Bible. It means a holy hush, i.e. a quieting of oneself before God. It is a solitary place. It is not speaking. It is not focusing on my problem. It is seeing God as did Isaiah in the sixth chapter of the book which bears his name. Satan will do all he can to disturb this, but it is here that we will again meet God.

The second meaning has the connotation of anticipation, i.e. not coming with a ho-hum attitude but with a belief and, if you will, an excitement that you know that things are right between you and God.

Thirdly, the word also means to have expectation. If I am indeed meeting God in the proper way, such as acknowledging my love for Him and my trust in Him, confessing my sins to Him, and trusting completely upon His mercy and grace, I can know that God is there.

The fourth meaning of wait, believe it or not, is *waiter*, one who is serving and waiting upon others. Beloved, this is such a key part of being renewed like an eagle in the time of my weariness. It means just keep doing what you know to do. Don't drop out of the race. Don't give in to your doubts and fears. Remember that if we are not weary in our well-doing in due time "we shall reap if we faint not," Galatians 6:9. It is here in this place of solitude that God will come with the provision of sufficiency and the promise of renewed strength. Of all that I have tried to say in this book, this is perhaps one of the most profound and enlightening truths that God has ever shared with me. It is here that I have the distinct privilege of coming boldly before His throne of grace that I might find grace to help in the hour of need.

Even in the Bible there are numerous opportunities to see tragedy in men who started well and then ran well only to give in to the race somewhere along the way.

You read of Aaron, of how faithful he was to God and to his brother Moses. Then because of the pressure of his ministry and because he did not pick his friends well, he gave in and lost his effectiveness. There was also David, Solomon, and Elijah, and on and on we could go. They all seemed to have a heart for God, but then did not fare well toward the end of their ministry, perhaps losing the best opportunities.

We must see God right up to the end. There is no time in this journey for the luxury of letting down our guard or becoming less intimate with the One (and only One) who can cause us to be the accomplisher of that which we have commenced; and that is God, and God alone. Kenneth Boa said, "We cannot follow Jesus when we are asking Him to follow us."[13] "We limit our spiritual development when we fail to make the transition from seeing Jesus as a problem solver to seeing Him as our life."[14]

Those of us who are senior ministers must be reminded again of Paul's admonition in Hebrews 12:12-13. *"Wherefore lift up the hands which hang down, and the feeble knees; and make straight paths for your feet, lest that which is lame be turned out of the way; but let it rather be healed."* We must never ever give the impression to those behind us that one can only run well or be victorious for a season, and then give in to the race. We must, by God's grace and help, prove our race by being faithful right up to the finish line.

May God help you to hear my heart in this chapter and feel my emotions in its lines. This has not been easy to write, but if it will keep just one of you from allowing the world, the flesh, and the devil from defeating you, it will all have been worthwhile.

Second Half of the Race

There seems to be an even greater temptation, after having been about a particular task a long period of time, to become less aggressive, less

---

[13] Boa, Kenneth; Conformed to His Image. Zondervan Publishing; Grand Rapids, Michigan. 2001 p. 66

[14] Ibid p. 249

motivated, and even—perhaps—less preoccupied than when we first began. Familiarity breeds more than contempt.

I don't know about you, but I have been quite discouraged as I have seen men older than myself in the ministry fall in later years to fear and temptations of all kinds. Men I looked up to and greatly admired. I have watched men whom I have tried to emulate and even worked at trying to be like, only to be let down as I have had to hear of their secret life and conduct that was so foreign to their message and calling.

I really thought that surely, the older we get, the less chance there is of Satan tempting us, sidetracking us or ultimately marring our testimony. However, now that I find myself in this time of life, I can tell you it just isn't so. From the cradle to the grave Satan has his ways, his tools, and his desires to cause us all to miss the mark. I only wish I would have had some older men tell me this as I began to enter these years. So I decided to at least jot down on paper some of my thoughts and warnings concerning what I will call, *Guarding weary Christians.*

"But none of these things move me, neither count I my life dear unto myself, so that I might finish my course with joy, and the ministry, which I have received of the Lord Jesus, to testify the gospel of the grace of God," Acts 20:24.

"Looking unto Jesus the author and finisher of our faith; who for the joy that was set before him endured the cross, despising the shame, and is set down at the right hand of the throne of God," Hebrews 12:2.

Scriptural Authority

Certainly, as we read this particular verse in the Bible in Hebrews 12:2, we do not learn that there will come a time when we will not need Jesus or perhaps not need him as much. We are told, however, that He is the one who began our faith (the author), and He is the finisher, the one who will bring us to the end. I think I did understand that, but again somehow I just thought the second half would kind of be a "home free" part of the race, a kind of downhill part of the race. It isn't. The same work is needed—the same faith, the same care, the same discipline. Allow me, in the next couple of pages to list some of the temptations I have experienced, with hope that it may alert you and make you cautious so as to be a finisher and not a beginner only.

Focus

A major temptation I have had to deal with as I run the second half of my race is in the area of focus. I had, and continue to have, difficulty keeping my mind and my eyes on the same objective that I had when I began.

Old age: after my 40th birthday, I started to think of my age more than I ever did before. I felt fine. I could still go out and run five miles three times a week and keep up with my daily schedule, really not noticing much more fatigue. However, time was beginning to take on new meaning. Jim Conway described time as an enemy, not a ally in his book, "Men in Midlife Crisis." "I was finding myself looking back with fond memories, but looking forward with sadness and even hoping the future would stay away. My age pressed on me, and I knew quite well the better half was over. The notions I had before, of always looking down the road, waiting for this event in life to come, was now left to the past. The future was dismal with weight gain, fatigue, graying hair, and balding."[15]

This, my friend, is a perfect set up of the devil. Any time he can get us anxious about the time of life in which we find ourselves, he has a greater potential to cause us to fail. The Bible warns us to be patient. Hebrews 10:36, *"For ye have need of patience, that, after ye have done the will of God, ye might receive the promise."*

A man, it seems, thrives on his manliness, his macho image. I don't think this is wrong as long as it is tempered by God. Certainly, God does not intend men to be wimps, or effeminate. He wants that male ego to be present. After all, that is what attracts him to the opposite sex. When he senses he is no longer as attractive as he was, it begins to hurt that male ego and, once again, here is where Satan sees his avenue for attack.

Many men, even men in the ministry, have become incredibly vulnerable because their focus has now shifted from the potential they have in Christ to the problems they are experiencing in the flesh. We feel that time is of an essence; we cannot wait too long or this flesh will be incapable of fulfilling our ambitions. Satan now has the stage set. Along comes a younger woman. She gives a compliment, makes a suggestion, and the man who at one time was strong in the Lord falls in disgrace and dishonor.

Satan has at last accomplished his work. What he could not accomplish in youth, he now accomplishes in the older stage of life.

---

[15] Conway, James. Men in Midlife Crisis. David C. Cook Publishing CO. Elgin, Il, 1978 p. 31

Suggestions

Time is as precious now as it ever was.

The Bible makes it very clear that man basically has an allotted time on this earth. When that day comes, we who know Christ will really begin to live.

The older we get, the more dependent we become upon others, especially on our Lord. None of us like to think of it, but it is a fact. We must face it, and face it with grace and dignity. Don't allow the devil to get you fearful and wavering in your faith. Go through the Psalms and Proverbs and notice how much is said concerning gray hair and age. Isaiah 46:4, *"And even to your old age I am He; and even to gray hairs will I carry you; I have made, and I will bear; even I will carry, and will deliver you."* Yes, if God was able to care for me in my early years, can He not care for me now and in my twilight years? Yes, He can! Yes, He will!

Before I move into another area of temptation, allow me to tell you this story. Soon after I was married, an insurance man came to our house with the intention of selling Gloria and me a policy. I remember him drawing a line on a piece of paper and saying, "David, between the two marks on this line you have the earning years. It is between these marks that you must make all the money you can. After you go past this mark, only the money you have made will sustain you in your old age." I cannot tell you how many times the devil has used that on me. He says to me, time and time again, "David, you'd better make money soon or it will be too late!" He wants to make me feel anxious, uneasy, impatient, and fearful.

Beloved, time is of an essence. We must use it wisely, but time is in God's hands. He who hath begun a good work in us wants to perform and complete it right up to the time of our departure. Let's trust Him even more in this stage of life. The song says, "He's always there, just when I need Him the most, just when I need Him the most."

Focus on the finish, not the flesh

Kenneth Boa tells the story of Eric Liddell's testimony in *Chariots of Fire*.

"Eric takes his sister Jenny for a walk in the hills of Scotland to explain his commitment to training for the 1924 Olympic games in Paris. He tells her, 'I've decided– I'm going back to China, the missionaries said I was accepted.' Jenny rejoiced to hear this, because she feared her brothers' calling to be a missionary was threatened by his interest in running. However Eric goes on, 'But I've got a lot of running to do first, Jenny–Jenny, you've got to understand. I believe that God made me for a purpose– for China. But, he also made me fast, and when I run, I feel his pleasure. To give it up would be to hold him in contempt. You were right–it's not just fun. To win is to honor Him.'"

Liddell was a man of focus and passion because he pursued a growing sense of God's purpose for his life. Frederick Buechner put it this way in *Wishful Thinking*, "The place God calls you to is the place where your deep gladness and the world's deep hunger meet."[16] When you are a

---

[16] Buechner, Frederick in Boa, Kenneth. Conformed to His Image. Zondervan Publishing ; Grand Rapids Michigan, 2001, p 249

person of a calling and purpose, your ultimate fulfillment will come when you finish that calling and purpose.

As I have already stated, it seems that the male ego is affected more in this area than the female. Man prides himself in his strength and with his competitive spirit, which is basically his image as a man. When he begins to sense a weakening of all this sometimes, if he is not careful, he will spend more time trying to salvage his body than sustaining his inner man. Many a good man has fallen into this temptation, including this writer.

As Satan gets our focus on the earthly rather than on the eternal, he will destroy us. By the Grace of God we must do all we can to maintain a healthy and fit body. But we must not allow our bodies to become our God and our focus. We must, because of the fact that we are not what we were physically, strive to be more spiritual than we have been in the past. This pattern must soon be laid down by many of us for the sake of the younger men coming up behind us. Just the other day, I was preaching in a Missions Conference with one of my senior heroes. One afternoon we decided to go out and spend the afternoon on the golf course. As we were riding in the golf cart to one of the holes, I said to this senior pastor, "Pastor, I want to personally thank you for being faithful to your Lord right up to this year." I could see tears well up in his eyes, and his chin began to quiver. He wanted to say something, but was unable. I think he was saying that it has always been a battle, but thank God for the victory!

By the grace of God, let's be especially careful in this part of the race. Let's somehow be as determined as was the Apostle Paul concerning not only beginning to run his race, but receiving the prize. I Corinthians 9:24,

"Know ye not that they who run in a race run all, but one receiveth the prize? So run, that ye may obtain." When Satan comes to your flesh, it unsettles you and tempts you. Somehow, keep your focus on the finish line. Don't allow a little pleasure, a little folding of the hands, to distract you from the completion of the race.

Just the other evening as I was preparing to return home after a Missions Conference, a newspaper in the hotel showed the picture of a young man having his mug-shot taken and being fingerprinted by the police. The article told how he and three of his friends had come to Florida for their Spring Break from college. While they were driving at high speed and under the influence of alcohol, he crashed his father's car and killed all three of his friends. He was now facing a minimum of 30 years in prison. When I looked more carefully at his photo, I could see he was just a boy, a scared young boy. Now, his life was changed forever. It seemed once again that the Spirit reminded me that, although this boy's life is a tragedy, there are so many men and women among God's people who, if they are not careful, will end up in spiritual tragedy with their lives altered for all time and eternity.

Yes, the second half of our race is every bit as important as was the first half. In fact, if you ever noticed in racing, the runners seem to be careful in the first part so as to be effective in the last. They conserve their energy; they plan ahead all the time. They certainly don't want to run well at first, only to be humiliated before the waiting crowd in the end.

The story is told about the Boston Marathon, which is a little over 26 miles long. Somewhere, approximately two-thirds through the race in Newton, Massachusetts, there is a hill known by runners as "Heartbreak

Hill." Properly called so, because it is here where—for many—the race is lost. It just seems to be the straw that breaks the camel's back. It is sad because once the runners get to the top, it is practically downhill from there on, but it is too much. Many of us experience the same. Instead of leaving behind us a legacy of goodness and the grace of God, we leave a pattern of sin, fatigue and failure.

My friends, you who are reading these lines are not home yet. Your race is not complete. It just might be that your particular trial is what God had pre-proposed to be your finest hour, your most profound testimony to those who are around you. Perhaps your greatest influence is right now. All the labors, all the joys, and the trials of the past were to bring you to this defining moment in time. Just like Joseph—who had enormous trials—left a legacy of trusting God that has impacted lives to this very hour, you too have a sphere of influence you must be careful not to neglect. May I humbly ask you again in closing? Are you so in love with your Lord and can you trust him in all his leadings to allow you to be a pattern, an example, to encourage others to fight the good fight of faith? God truly works in mysterious ways His wonders to perform.

CPSIA information can be obtained at www.ICGtesting.com
Printed in the USA
BVOW012209200812

298317BV00001B/8/P